For Marye Campbell,
With my best wishes.
Happy stitching!
Phyllis Kluger

April 26. 1976

A Needlepoint Gallery of

PATTERNS FROM THE PAST

A Needlepoint Gallery of PATTERNS FROM THE PAST

by PHYLLIS KLUGER

Alfred A. Knopf

New York 1975

THIS IS A BORZOI BOOK
PUBLISHED BY ALFRED A. KNOPF, INC.

Library of Congress Cataloging in Publication Data

Kluger, Phyllis.
    Patterns from the past.

    1. Canvas embroidery—Patterns. I. Title.
TT778.C3K59   746.4′4   75-8234

Manufactured in the United States of America

First Edition

For Richard

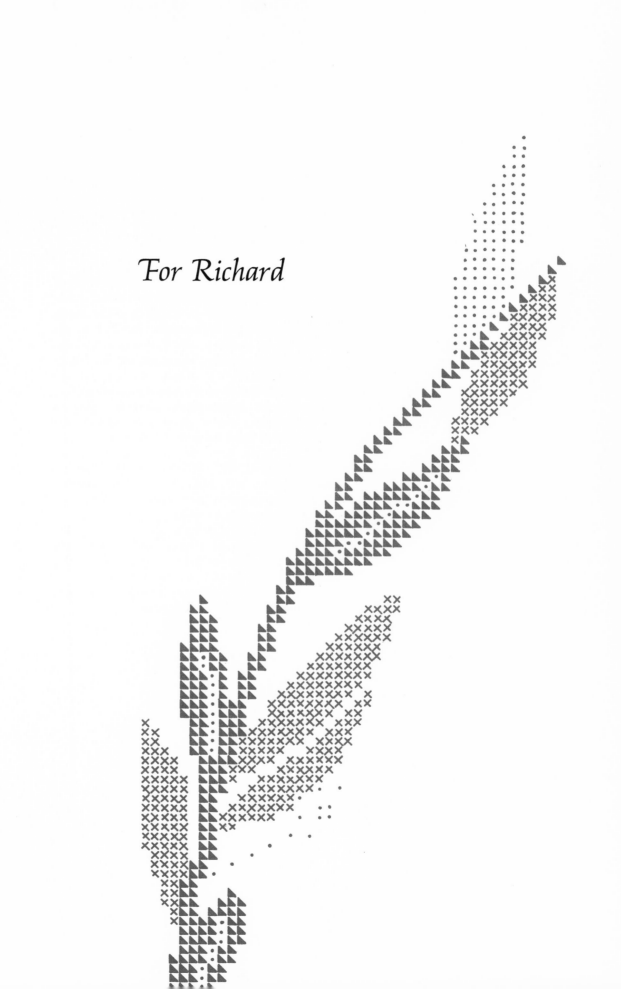

ACKNOWLEDGMENTS

SEVERAL PEOPLE have helped in the preparation of this book, contributing to it in large and small ways. Among those I would like to thank are the many teachers whose wisdom and insight instilled in me the desire to go on learning; the Trustees of Columbia University, whose policy of permitting graduates to return to its libraries is deeply appreciated; my editor, Robert Gottlieb, whose enthusiasm helped fuel my efforts; and my agents John Cushman and Jane Wilson. I would also like to thank Mrs. Jay D. Arbeiter, Mrs. David Baer, Mrs. B. W. Bowie, Mr. and Mrs. John K. Doyle, Mrs. Stanley Friedman, Mrs. Lawrence Goodman, Mr. and Mrs. Arthur Kessler, Mrs. Mark Kweller, Mrs. Michael Manning, Maurice Sendak, and my mother, Mrs. Samuel Rubin, who taught me to work with a needle.

Special thanks must be given to Helen Barrow, who devoted vast amounts of energy and time to the countless details that comprised the production of this volume.

My husband, Richard Kluger, helped me in more ways than it is possible to enumerate.

Contents

Introduction

FOR THE NEEDLEPOINT DEVOTEE, the act of pulling a threaded needle through a piece of heavy fabric over and over again brings comfort and joy. More of the former, perhaps, for most of us, who normally occupy ourselves in an often tense, high-powered environment (whether office, factory, or home) and find in needlepoint a welcome, relaxing release that permits us to unwind while making something lovely. Since creativity is not normally thought of as a depressurizing process, needlepoint is a rare blending of craft with therapy.

If it serves no further function, then, this book is intended to provide 102 patterns inspired by the great art of the past that, in themselves, should offer pleasure to the needlepointer who executes them, and a corresponding joy to those who behold the finished renderings. There is a further purpose aspired to here: to encourage the needleworker to become self-sufficient and thus more creative in choosing designs.

If the canvas is bought already painted and colored for you, you can of course derive gratification from executing the pattern, as I hope you shall from the ones in this book. But working a pre-designed canvas means that someone else has done the initial job of selecting, thinking about, and visualizing the way the finished product should look. By making an emotional investment in the act of buying an empty canvas and then finding the subject and technique with which to fill it, you are joined in the creative process from the beginning; you are performing the dual role of artist *and* craftsman—surely a greater satisfaction. To execute subjects of acknowledged artistic merit, to focus attention on details never before perceived—to look at the trees instead of the forest, for a change—can bring emotional gratification on many levels. This was true for me, at any rate, because in examining the art of the past and adapting it for a medium that I enjoy working in, I was forced to learn a lot, not only about art, but about my craft and, as an unexpected by-product, myself. The process was often arduous and time-consuming but it was, above all, exciting. I strongly recommend it to others.

This collection of designs is built upon ten periods of time. Each marks a more or less discrete historical epoch in the massive monument known loosely as Western art. The beginning and terminal dates of each, especially the ancient eras, are necessarily hazy, and the groupings here of several major periods under one catch-all label is of course arbitrary. But at least a general pattern and method are intended to be at work, displaying in approximately chronological order a sampling of many of the great motifs that have survived over the centuries. Art is a cumulative process, working its way deep into mankind's historical subconscious, and so an effort has been made to illustrate a procession of the patterns beginning with the ancient prototypes that—perhaps in different colors, perhaps in inspired variation—have come enduringly and freshly alive to successive times and places and civilizations. A number of the designs gathered here are unique to their own age and are all the more intriguing for that fact. (Intentionally omitted are motifs from twentieth-century art, not because the modern period is not a rich one but because it is so overwhelmingly with us all the time in the images that we see on television and movie screens, billboards and slick-paper magazines, soap boxes and coffee tins.)

The designs in the collection were selected on the basis of their adaptability to needlepoint canvas, a two-dimensional, flat surface. I therefore tried to limit myself to designs that were conceived as flat surfaces so that the spirit of the artist's original intention (or at least what posterity conceives it to have been) could be maintained. I admit to having occasionally "flattened out" some three-dimensional conceptions for the sake of the design potential inherent in the form, but in general I attempted to avoid that sort of tampering. Subjects with clearly defined edges and strong linear values are the easiest to translate from art work to needlepoint canvas. A Matisse collage, for example, works better than a Matisse painting, because in the former there is no attempt to violate or break through the medium in which the artist chose to express himself, nor does one necessarily have to lose a major element of the artist's statement— the way in which he chose to apply his pigment to the canvas.

The collection comprises three different kinds of designs: (1) repetitive motifs that can be extended to any length vertically and horizontally; (2) single motifs that can be used alone, or repeated, if one likes, but are a discrete entity; and (3) a border pattern that can be used either vertically or horizontally, repeated or not to frame a center design or be used alone. All that is required of you, the needlepointer, is a bit of imagination in order to envision the way these motifs might appear in the shades and sizes of your choice.

The genesis of this collection was both personal fulfillment and a need to economize. Shortly after I had begun to learn the basics of needlepoint, I discovered that the cost of purchasing handpainted canvases was often beyond my means. Unpainted canvas was relatively cheap, as was the yarn to cover it, especially when bought by the ounce, and leftover yarn from one project could be saved and used in others. There was, however, one problem. I have never had great artistic ability; in fact, my drawing talent is really quite minimal. So I could not paint my own canvases. The problem was to find designs suitable to needlepoint canvas and a means of transferring them to the surface.

At the time, I was an art history student, and it took me some years to realize that the best needlepoint designers were there in front of me. As a knitter, I had worked designs from graphs, and it occurred to me that I might use graph paper on which to reproduce some of the motifs I was exposed to every day in my studies. At first I did little sketches in the margins of my notebooks—notes for future reference. My sketches, though, were not accurate—they were done in haste, after all—and the remarks scribbled beside them (e.g., "four triangles meeting within") didn't help much. But a few minutes spent in the library with photographs, tracing paper, and a pencil did. With the whole library to play with, I was home free.

Soon I decided that to re-create an entire painting on canvas— The Last Supper in needlepoint, for example—was a malefaction. An abomination, even. If Leonardo had wanted a tapestry, he would have woven one himself. A work of art, especially a painting, should not be translated into another medium, I believe, because it does not do justice to the original. Technique and subtlety, those elusive qualities that elevate a painting to a work of art, to a masterpiece, are completely lost, and what one then has is a low-quality reproduction, badly drawn and poorly colored. There are, therefore, no complete works in this collection, only details, and even these may have been consciously amended somewhat in the adaptation.

All of the designs were deliberately executed with materials available locally at small shops—Persian three-ply yarns with monocanvas of ten, thirteen, or fourteen threads to the inch. In all cases where number 10 (ten threads to the inch) canvas was used, the captions so indicate. The metallic yarns I occasionally used were those manufactured under the Elsa Williams Needlecraft label, which, I believe, has wide distribution. It may be overly bright for some tastes, and if so, woolen yarn can be substituted. Stitches were restricted to a simply executed few because design was more important to me than texture. I have found that small stitches tend to wear better than those carried over long stretches of canvas, and so have executed these pieces accordingly; I would hate to see a zipper catch in a long thread, and the havoc it would wreak on something that had taken months to achieve.

The choice of designs within any one period of Western art history is purely subjective. I selected the kinds of things I thought I would enjoy doing and that I thought others might. There were other considerations that had to be met (principal among them, size) because I wanted to include for each design a chart that was legible enough so that a magnifying glass would be unnecessary. In order to achieve the greatest variety possible, I have tried to search out and include designs that were relatively obscure—and therefore "fresh" to the modern eye—as well as a few inspired by more familiar works.

I have not included a rating for the degree of difficulty of any of the designs because I feel that if the chart of a design is readily understood (especially when compared with the photograph of that design), the pattern is relatively easy to do. In general, if the pattern is small and repetitive, it is easier to execute than a large, irregular pattern requiring many changes of shape and color.

Before each group of designs there is a brief discussion of some of the social and historical forces acting upon the artists who originally produced the work. This book does not pretend to be a thumbnail history of art; it is offered simply as a gallery of design based on memorable artistic works of the past. The caption descriptions contain a bit of background information about the work from which the design is derived, and sometimes a little more when it seemed especially fascinating. Knowing something about the origin of a design seems to make the design more authentic and significant; history can endow a work with more meaning than its surface alone can convey. The information also provides an element of delight to anyone executing it that might otherwise be lost. Isn't that, after all, the reason we do needlepoint?

SOME (NOT VERY) TECHNICAL POINTS

THERE ARE NO REFERENCES HERE to any specific hues, partly because the printing inks used to produce color are chemically different from the yarn dyes and there may be some degree of distortion. All of the shades shown will therefore have to be approximations, just as the yarns themselves are approximations of the artists' own pigments. I have seen some of the original works alluded to in this collection, but for others I have had to rely on reproductions, which are not always very accurate. Seeing the original work is unfortunately no guarantee of accuracy of hue because color tends to be a function of light, which varies even within a museum, depending on the time of day, the kind of lighting, the outside weather conditions, and so on. One should always place quotation marks around all uses of the word "original" throughout this collection when it appears in a discussion of color, because in some cases I have had to rely on the eyes of others, archaeological reports, reprints, and other forms of color reproduction. In general, almost all of the shades shown are brighter than the original hues, for I have used commercial needlepoint yarns that are chemically dyed and are more highly saturated than natural pigment would likely be, especially after the passage of time.

I use the words "adapted from" and "derived from" rather loosely throughout the book, for in many cases the work of art served only as the starting point for a design that may in fact look quite different from the original. The gap may not necessarily be very wide, but in the process of regularizing motifs for needlepoint some changes were inevitable.

The stitches employed have been kept simple. This book was not conceived of as a needlepoint primer, of which there are many already in existence, but for people who know basic techniques and are interested in discovering new ways to use them. A sophisticated knowledge of stitchery is not required in order to execute these patterns. The most familiar one, the continental (or tent) stitch, is used most frequently here. The basketweave stitch, which produces the same effect on the surface as the continental, may also be used. Both stitches produce a heavy padding on the reverse side of the canvas; this is necessary if the piece is going to receive hard use, as with a pillow or a chair seat. If one intends to frame the needlepoint, the half cross stitch done in the "stab" technique, which leaves little yarn on the reverse side, may be used instead. The bargello stitch, or a slight variation of it, is also used throughout the book, though to a lesser degree. (I have used the name "bargello stitch" to describe the long, vertical stitch that usually covers four threads of the canvas instead of the less familiar terms "Hungarian point," or "Florentine stitch," or anything else because that is the one that, accurately or not, is given widest currency.) In a few examples, other stitches are also used; the charts that accompany each design indicate how these other stitches are to be done in a way that I hope will be clear to the reader. In any case, continental stitches covering the same number of threads in the canvas as the fancy stitches can always be substituted.

Some designs in this collection use a combination of continental and bargello stitches. Where the two are used together, it is usually easier to do the bargello work first. Follow it with the continental stitches, pulling up the bargello stitches slightly in order to slide the continental stitches beneath them at the edges where the two join. In this way the canvas will be completely covered.

The charts have been designed to be as clear as possible, and should be easily understood so long as the following points are kept in mind. (1) In designs using only continental stitches, each typographical symbol on the chart represents one continental stitch. (2) In designs that use only bargello stitches, the lines superimposed on the graph background represent the stitches; the graph lines should be read as threads of the canvas. (3) In designs that use both kinds of stitches, continental as well as bargello, the small diagonal lines (or other easily recognizable symbols) represent continental stitches, the long vertical (or horizontal) lines represent bargello stitches. If a larger version of a design is desired, one can simply use canvas of a larger mesh size.

Although I used canvas of only three sizes, most of the designs can be done on any size canvas. Most of the charts can also be used in many other media where individual units are used to create a large design: knitting, cross-stitch, and latch-hooked rugs, for example. I have only one caveat, and that is if bargello stitches are very long, they are more apt to catch on zippers, hangnails, or some other wayward snag, so it is best to keep bargello work on number 13 canvas or a smaller size (remember that canvas numbers refer to threads per inch; the larger the number of a canvas, the smaller each individual stitch on that canvas will be).

When executing a pattern, I find it easier to outline a shape first and fill it in afterward. Remember, too, when doing a symmetrical pattern to check the sides against each other frequently to make sure they match. Ripping out work is no fun.

Some of the designs in the collection consist of vertical or horizontal motifs, which can be used for belts, drapery tiebacks, or bell pulls, should one have need of these. If not, the motifs can be repeated vertically or horizontally on the same piece of canvas until the desired size for a pillow, foot stool, chair seat, or whatever is reached. Some of the designs may seem most suitable for framing; a small grouping of four or five, for example, might be effective. There are no specific suggestions given for the use of any of the patterns here because each person will envision the application of a pattern differently. There is, as there should be, enormous freedom of choice; there are no recommendations for "projects." One may, of course, combine the motifs and pieces of motifs in any number of ways, changing the colors, mixing a pattern from the eighteenth century A.D., for example, with one from the eighteenth century B.C. Artists have done just that all through history, turning to the past for inspiration; but somehow they were able to reinterpret what they found for their own time and needs and, in the process, to create something entirely new.

THE "HOW" OF IT

THERE ARE SEVERAL METHODS for transferring the design you have selected to the canvas.

1. Find a friend with a photo studio and an enlarger. Bring him or her a black-and-white photo of the design you wish to stitch and ask that it be enlarged 20, 50, 200 percent, or whatever. The more it is enlarged, the greater detail you'll be able to achieve in your rendering of the design. Then take a piece of canvas, place it over the enlarged black-and-white photo and, with acrylic or oil paint, trace the outlines of the design onto the canvas and fill in the details, too. Acrylic paint tends to dry faster than oil but the important thing is that both be waterproof. Never, *never* use anything but waterproof materials on canvas—when blocked, the color will run and you'll be furious and saddened. I do not have a friend with a photo studio, although during the course of this work I often wished I had. My job would have been easier. Instead I improvised as follows:

2. Buy graph paper in several sizes. I have four—8 squares to the inch, 10 squares to the inch, 5 squares to the centimeter (which works out to about 13 squares to the inch), and 10 millimeters to the centimeter (or about 25 squares per inch). College bookstores tend to have the largest and most varied assortment, but office supply establishments are usually adequate. Visibility is extremely important to me, so I use the 10-millimeter paper only in dire emergencies (see below). My staple is 10-squares-to-the-inch paper. The squares are big enough to be seen easily and the paper contains enough of them so that it is usually not necessary to paste two or more sheets together.

I take a fresh piece of this paper and place the design I want to use alongside it. Then I sketch the design directly onto the paper. Lightly. In pencil. I make the drawing big enough so that each stitch of the outline will occupy one square of the graph paper. This means that I have to pay close attention to details before I even begin because the details are often what sets the scale for the entire shape. Sometimes I have to paste sheets of graph paper together in order to get everything in.

Next I look at what I've done. If the shape is too fat here or too thin there, I erase my sketchy line and try again. And again. And many more times, if necessary. Sometimes I am given help by an encouraging spouse: "Your bottom is a little too thick." Or by a passing child: "A horse doesn't have such a thin neck and its legs are longer and its tail sticks out like *that*—and you've made the stomach wrong."

It helps occasionally to turn your sketch, as well as whatever you're sketching from, upside down in order to gain a new perspective. Or you can abandon it for a few hours and try again later. Eventually you'll come upon a satisfactory outline. At that point I take my pencil and start X-ing in the squares that will form the outline of the design. Just an X in each graph paper square. When finished, I look very hard at the paper because a thick, definite X looks different from a thin, sketchy line, and the proportions between elements of a design can change slightly in the process. If not satisfied, I erase and try again, moving the outline up, down, out, or whatever, trying to keep in mind that stitches, especially continental stitches, are tiny, diagonal lines, not the chunky squares of the paper.

When the outline is X-ed in, take a pen and ink in the outlined squares. A large dot will do. A large selection of colored pens will help you to approximate the hues of the finished work right on the graph paper.

I must admit that this method is usually not mastered overnight and will take much practice to achieve satisfactory results. For a beginner, the method works best with small geometric patterns consisting of shapes with 90- or 45-degree angles. Curves especially require some degree of facility, since at best they can only be approximate. Remember that you're in the process of training yourself and that, barring divine inspiration, there is no substitute for practice. Some people will, unfortunately, never perfect it to their own satisfaction.

Now for the "dire emergency" mentioned above. If you are not an artist and *cannot* draw well enough even with help and great patience, you might try something else. This is what I did for the small rabbit in the Renaissance section (see page 143): The image I wanted to adapt was tiny—it measured less than two inches in width. I took a piece of tracing paper, placed it over the picture, and got an outline of the animal. Next I put the traced outline over a sheet of carbon paper with the 10-millimeter paper directly underneath it. I then drew over the traced outline, reproducing it on the paper. At that point I picked up my magnifying glass, gritted my teeth, and transposed the pattern square for square from the smaller graphed paper to the 10-squares-to-the-inch paper. It was painstaking, patience-wearing, and annoying. But it worked. I then had a perfect outline for the rabbit. Sketching in the shades of gray was hopscotch after that.

This tracing-and-carbon-paper method works even better if you have no desire to change the scale. Just trace the outline, place over carbon paper, draw it directly onto graph paper in the scale of canvas you intend to use, X in the outline—and you're all set. You did not have to sketch a single line.

The
NEEDLEPOINT GALLERY
in COLOR

The number below each design on the following twenty pages refers to the specific page, later in the book, on which the general discussion and graphed chart of the design are to be found.

These needlepoint designs have been grouped according to their artistic period or cultural association, and appear in approximate chronological order. Brief commentaries sketching the historical and artistic trends of the periods precede each grouping. The patterns have been executed, for the most part, in shades closely resembling those used by the original artists, but it must be remembered that these hues are themselves only approximations. The reader is therefore urged to experiment, to seek and combine whatever colors elicit her or his own personal delight.

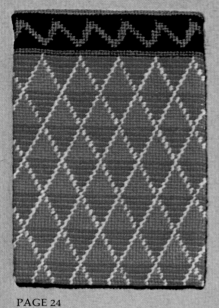

PAGE 24

I
DESIGNS FROM THE ART OF THE
MINOANS

PAGE 19

PAGE 30

PAGE 23

PAGE 20

PAGE 24

PAGE 28

PAGE 26

PAGE 31

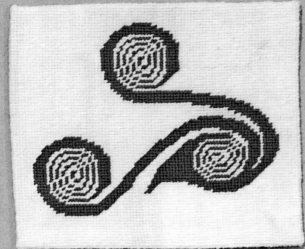

PAGE 22

II
DESIGNS FROM THE ART OF
ANCIENT EGYPT

PAGE 36

PAGE 35

PAGE 38

PAGE 37

PAGE 41

PAGE 40

PAGE 43

PAGE 42

PAGE 44

PAGE 46

PAGE 51

PAGE 52

PAGE 53

PAGE 54

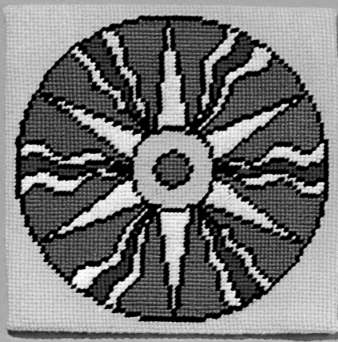

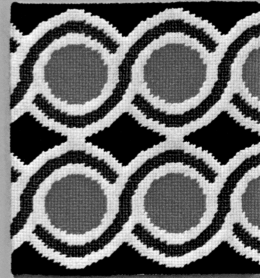

PAGE 56

PAGE 57

III
DESIGNS FROM THE ART OF THE
ANCIENT NEAR EAST

PAGE 58

PAGE 60

PAGE 61

PAGE 62

IV
DESIGNS FROM THE ART OF
GREECE AND ROME

PAGE 67

PAGE 68

PAGE 70

PAGE 74

PAGE 72

PAGE 75

PAGE 73

PAGE 76

PAGE 78

PAGE 80

V   DESIGNS FROM
THE ART OF THE
BYZANTINE EMPIRE

PAGE 85

PAGE 91

PAGE 86

PAGE 87

PAGE 88

PAGE 90

PAGE 102

PAGE 96

PAGE 97

PAGE 100

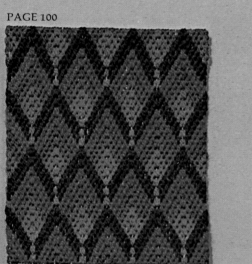

PAGE 101

PAGE 94

PAGE 107

VI
DESIGNS FROM THE ART OF THE
MIDDLE AGES

PAGE 110

PAGE 108

PAGE 109

PAGE 112

PAGE 114

PAGE 118

PAGE 116

PAGE 119

PAGE 120

VII
DESIGNS FROM THE ART OF
ISLAM

PAGE 125

PAGE 136

VIII
DESIGNS FROM THE ART OF THE
RENAISSANCE

PAGE 140

PAGE 139

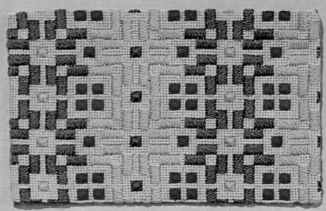

PAGE 144

PAGE 142

PAGE 148

PAGE 150

PAGE 143

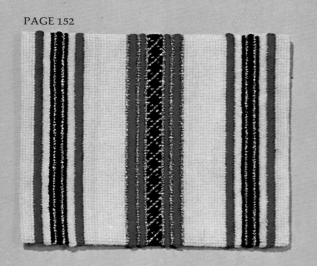

PAGE 152

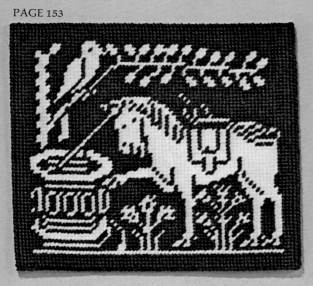

PAGE 153

PAGE 154

IX
DESIGNS FROM THE ART OF
17th–19th Century EUROPE

PAGE 159

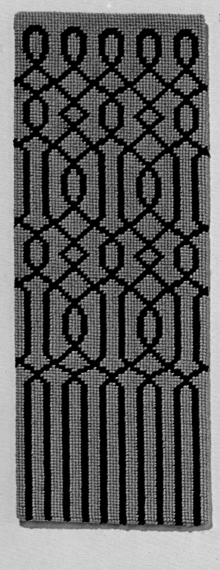

PAGE 160

PAGE 164

PAGE 162

PAGE 165

PAGE 166

PAGE 167

PAGE 168

PAGE 170

PAGE 171

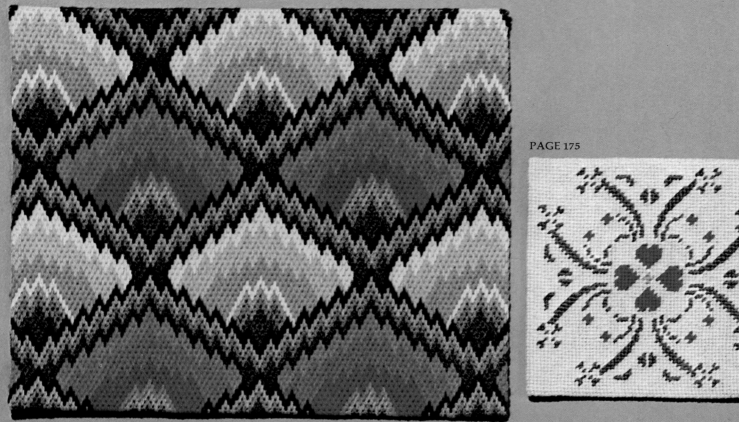

PAGE 175

PAGE 176

PAGE 178

PAGE 184

N°240

PAGE 180

PAGE 182

PAGE 186

PAGE 181

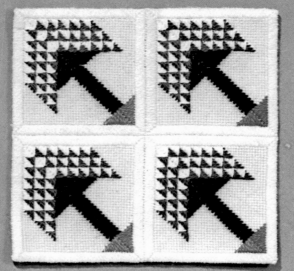

PAGE 188

PAGE 190

I DESIGNS FROM THE ART OF THE MINOANS

PERHAPS the most appealing of all ancient designs are those executed by the Cretans (or the Minoans, as they are also called, after the legendary King Minos). More than 150 miles long and only one fifth as wide, Crete looks like a great canoe afloat in the eastern Mediterranean. The island was a place of dramatic contrasts—stony mountain ranges topped by snow-crowned Mount Ida, her 8,000-foot-high silhouette a beacon to mariners; lush forest stands of cypress much in demand in nearby Egypt; and sandy beaches that formed countless natural harbors. The climate was gentle, and abundant rainfall, gushing springs, and flowing rivers nourished the plains of the island and made it fertile with olive trees and flora in rich profusion. Even the summer heat, notoriously fierce in that part of the world, was moderated by the prevailing northerly winds. Most important of all, though, was the sea in conditioning the manner and quality of people's lives. The sea was all around them, visible from almost any rise. It nurtured them and protected them like a vast moat from the threat of marauding invaders. And it brought them wealth, for their island was a maritime crossroads, anchored almost midway between the three great continents of Europe, Asia, and Africa.

Blessed by nature and geography, the Cretans had little need to devote their energies to self-protection —the consuming occupation of so many ancient peoples. Instead they focused their attention on the manifestations of nature that they saw around them, on people, animals, and plants. As a result their designs are infused with an exuberant energy derived from close observation; the forms never seem to be at rest. They move, change direction, and even appear to sprout like palpably growing wildlife.

Many of the designs that follow are adapted from wall decorations found in the palace at Knossos, the capital of ancient Crete. These decorations are, for the most part, true frescoes, executed in the same technique that was used three millennia later by Renaissance masters: plastering the surface to be decorated and applying pigment to the wet plaster. The colors penetrate into the surface and become fixed as they dry, so that even today, in the museum at Herakleion, Crete's principal city, where the original plaster fragments have been taken and whole scenes restored, the colors remain fresh, bright, and clear.

What can be called Minoan civilization began around 2600 B.C., and its art, like that of all peoples, developed gradually. Among the first relics we have are lightly carved stone vases and pottery fragments with linear designs incised into them. Occasionally a white powder would be rubbed into the incisions to produce a light-on-dark effect. This earliest period lasted for about four centuries, and it was only during the succeeding era that the spiral pattern, which was to become the characteristic element of Cretan art, was first seen on pottery.

Used first on the Cycladic Islands just north of Crete in the Aegean Sea, the spiral motif, at first just a series of interlocking C forms, evolved into more complex connections of S and Z shapes, until many designs were used that were based loosely on the swastika—an angular spiral and a sacred astral or solar symbol to the Minoans. It is a design element that can be found throughout the art of many peoples, from the Orient to the American Indians. There are several designs in this section in which the swastika or a variation of it can readily be seen.

Minoan wall frescoes are charged with a vitality that cannot be found anywhere in the ancient world. Flying fish, a stalking cat, a leaping deer, and a crocus-picking monkey were all subjects for the Cretan artist who delighted in their motion. The large central panels were rich in human and plant depictions, too. Stately, wasp-waisted men, and gesturing, bare-breasted women seated at a sacred gathering were painted with startling animation. Even the Minoan bull leapers, boys and girls who supposedly engaged in a ritual act that included grasping a charging bull by the horns and flipping over its body to land on their feet again, are depicted unafraid in their joyous mobility. The same lyric quality of motion and vitality was applied to the border patterns that surrounded the larger works. Though often rather abstract, the forms take on an organic quality—they seem to move, to sprout, to grow, radiating outward like plants twisting in their quest for the sun. Ceilings, too, were often frescoed, and here the Cretans were particularly inventive. Because they were aware that a ceiling would be seen from many different directions, there is no "top" or "bottom" to the paintings; they can be viewed equally well from any vantage point.

The palace at Knossos, the largest of all the Cretan structures, was a fairly huge complex. As much as four stories high, it was composed of rooms of various sizes and functions—chambers of state measuring 42 by 48 feet, apartments for royalty and their retinue of servants, workshops, and storerooms. It also contained an ingenious network of pipes and roof cisterns that provided running water for the sinks and flushing toilets. The largest pipes, the effluent channels, were provided with manholes to permit cleaning. Even a few painted terra-cotta bathtubs were found at the site. The Minoans were not only accomplished artists and architects but also engineers and plumbers.

Just as Minoan art in general exhibits an organic quality, so the principal architectural monument of the civilization is an example of organic growth. Originally the palace began as a cluster of small buildings that were grouped around a series of courtyards. As the population increased in size, so did the palace. The spaces between the buildings and courtyards were roofed over and formed the supporting story for the level above—a process of gradual accretion that continued until the structure resembled a labyrinth, or maze. The word "labyrinth" is of Cretan, or pre-Greek, derivation; a *labrys* was a double-headed ax, depictions of which were found throughout the palace at Knossos. Thus the labyrinth, or palace of the *labrys*, came to mean a maze, with its complicated, tortuous turnings through rooms, hallways, stairways, and courtyards until finally the exit was reached.

Because of the warm climate of the island and the fierce brilliance of the light, there were few exterior windows in the palace. Light wells were used instead —shafts or narrow inner courtyards that pierced the building from the basement through the various floors and were open at the roof. Rooms in the palace were provided with interior windows and porticos that, in turn, opened out on these shafts, thus allowing indirect light and fresh air to enter them by means of the light wells. In this way, the inside of the palace was protected from the heat of the sun but was also rather dimly lit; for this reason it is likely that many of the designs derived from Cretan frescoes are so brightly, almost gaudily, colored.

▲ ▲

By 1500 B.C., the brilliance of Cretan art had diminished to a fitful glow, perhaps because of the invasion of the island by early Greeks. Homes at Knossos were abandoned and the palace itself was damaged. The blow was not fatal, but it was indeed a prefiguration. A century later, the palace at Knossos was destroyed by an as yet unknown, perhaps greater than human force. Because of the geological instability of the eastern Mediterranean area, the island of Crete has been subject, even up to modern times, to earthquakes and tremors great and small. It may be that the earth itself trembled and shook, and forever ended the Minoan celebration of life.

MINOAN POTTERY DESIGNS were initially very simple. A few lines or chevrons that seem almost random in their placement appear on most of the artifacts that have been found. This design, however, is sophisticated, with its opposing diagonal and horizontal lines forming framed, interlocking triangles. In such early pottery the lines were incised into the clay and then a whitish powder was rubbed into the incisions before firing to produce a pattern of light gray on dark gray. The colors were, of course, changed in this adaptation, and the use of the continental stitch tends to soften somewhat the sharp opposition of the diagonals. This design has a universal quality similar to the sort of geometric arrangement found in the art of China, Africa, and among the American Indians.

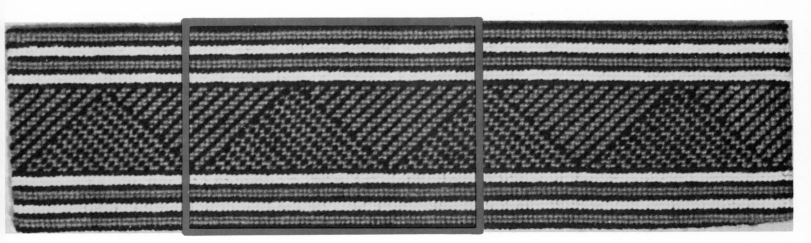

ACTUAL SIZE 12¼" × 3¼"

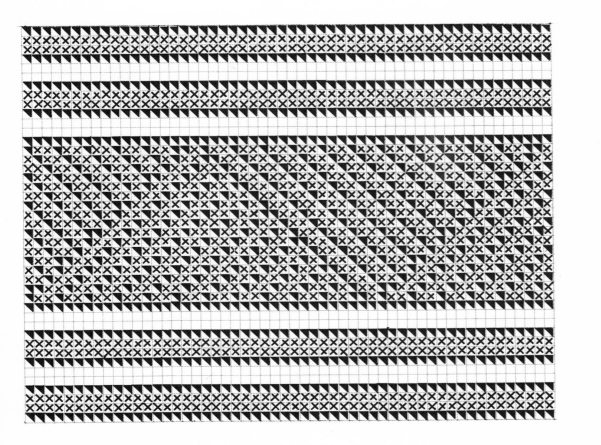

◥ BLACK
✕ RED
☐ WHITE

ACTUAL SIZE 7" × 11⅜"

THOUGH THE CRETANS often decorated cere-
monial rooms with large wall frescoes, occasionally
they used only a patterned band around the upper
walls. One such band is reproduced here close in size
to the original that contains the Minoans' favorite
motif, the spiral. The colors, primary hues plus black
and white, are brilliant in combination and must have
provided the viewer with a reminder of summer
flowers on a damp, chilly winter day.

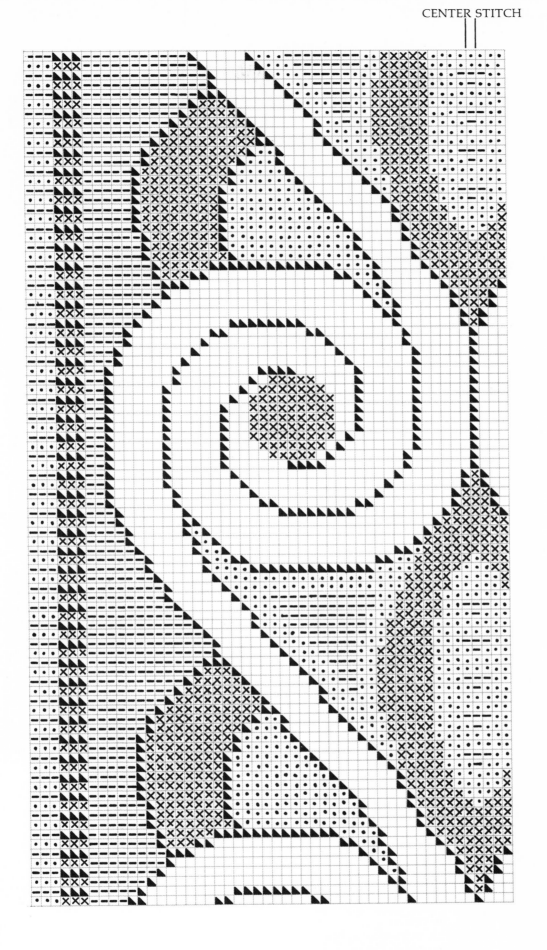

□ WHITE
▲ BLACK
✕ BLUE
– RED
• YELLOW

21

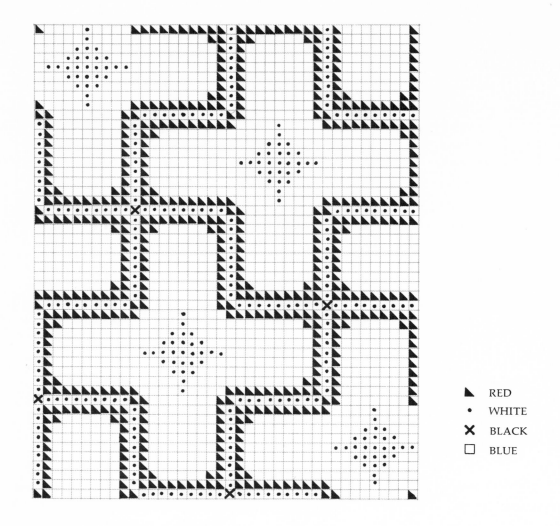

▶ RED
• WHITE
✖ BLACK
☐ BLUE

THE CRUCIFORM appeared frequently in Minoan textiles. This design was found at Knossos in a fresco of Minoan men dressed in their usual daily attire of short, patterned kilts. Slightly different crosslike patterns are seen in the kilts of the other men in the painting. This particular design is distinguished by the right-angled lines that form swastikas, that favored Minoan motive, into which the crosses are set. Every section of the right-angled lines was marked by the black dots that are reproduced in this design, and the resulting diagonals counterpoint the ninety-degree angularity.

ACTUAL SIZE 6¼" × 7"

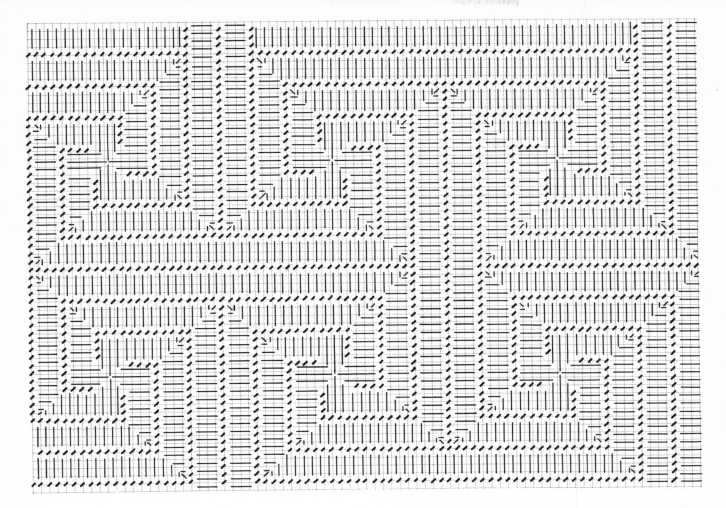

✎ TERRA COTTA

| YELLOW

THIS LABYRINTH PATTERN was painted on a wall in the palace above a dado, or lower wall painting, that depicted rocks—a kind of artificial marbling, perhaps. We can only speculate if this might have been a kind of shorthand, or symbol, of the structure, since it was set near a rocky mountain range. The design was originally painted as it has been reproduced here—in reddish brown on a yellow ground. The long bargello stitches used in the ground between the lines produce a textured effect as they change direction. In the design shown here, contrary to others in this book, it is easier to execute the continental stitches first and follow with the bargello work. The chart indicates the length and arrangement of the bargello stitches in the center of the motif.

ACTUAL SIZE 6" × 8"

THE CHARACTERISTIC CRETAN SPIRAL is multiplied by four here. This pattern has been somewhat simplified from the original because its source was a painted stucco relief ceiling. That is, the arms of the spirals and the flower-like forms between them were molded in plaster and then applied to the ceiling, thus creating a three-dimensional effect. When dry, the plaster was painted. A bit of artistic license has been taken with the Minoan design, for the original contained a smaller proportion of red. To enhance the swirling effect of the spiral (and because the three-dimensionality of the original could not be reproduced effectively in needlepoint), alternate arms are executed in red here. The red and white, a scheme used in many Minoan frescoes, results in a checkerboard effect.

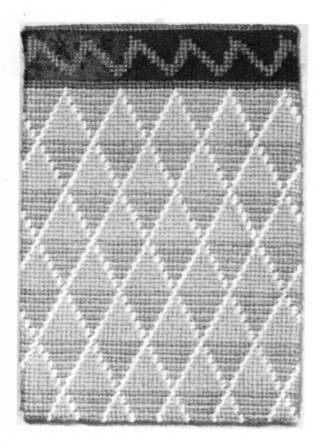

IT IS FITTING for this design to be executed in needlepoint, for it is believed to have been an embroidery pattern that was reproduced in a fresco. The design was found in a painting depicting a procession of women dressed in bright, flounced skirts. Presumably, each of the ruffled tiers of the skirt had a contrasting border at its hem. (There may have been as many as five separate descending ruffles to Minoan skirts, for an ivory statuette of a goddess in the Boston Museum of Fine Arts has five gold bands around the skirt.) The flounce and its border are in the original colors.

The enormous artistic ability of the Minoans may be seen even here, and one wonders if at such an early date (ca. 1650 B.C.) the relationships of the modern color wheel were already known. To use black and blue next to orange and white, to intensify the brilliance of a color by using its opposite, or complementary, is artistic sophistication on an advanced level. One is fascinated, too, by how the artist took half the lozenge, or diamond shape, found in the skirt and curved and stylized its lines to make a second variation on the theme of the zig-zag.

ACTUAL SIZE 4⅞" × 7⅛"

BLACK
BLUE
RED
YELLOW
WHITE

LIGHT ORANGE
RED-ORANGE
BLACK
BLUE
WHITE

25

THE FRESCO TECHNIQUE requires that the painter work with great speed and accuracy, for the plaster onto which he applies the pigment dries very quickly. Under such conditions, lines and squares incised into the plaster would be useful aids. Such lines have been found in bits of plaster by archaeologists. This example from a ceiling fresco is one pattern that might have been squared off. The tiny black dots in the center of each yellow circle are equidistant from one another and might easily have served as markers to the painter, who could have used them as guideposts. Because this design was executed on a ceiling, the leaf pattern would be seen right side up from any part of the room—there is no "up" or "down" in the pattern. Some scholars believe that what we see as a leaf shape was in actuality the Minoan symbol for a tree (the veins may readily be regarded as branches), and it may have been, as it was to many groups in the ancient Near East, a sacred symbol of fertility.

ACTUAL SIZE 13¼" × 9⅛"

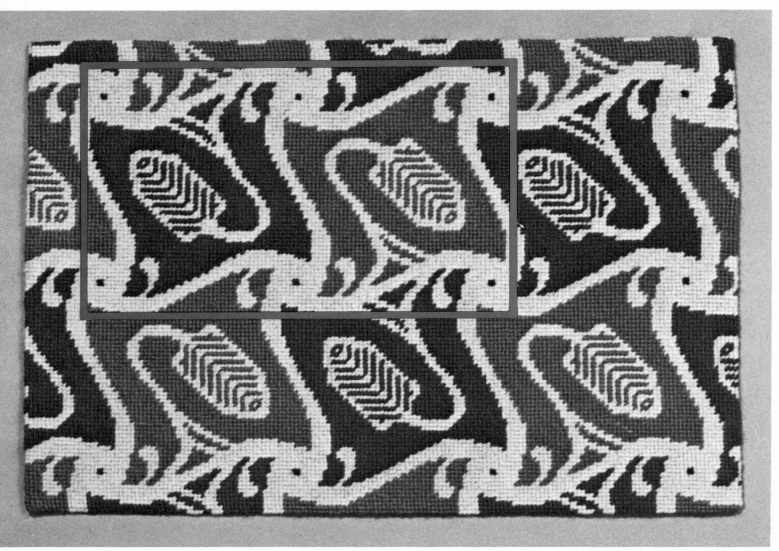

▲ BLUE
∠ RED
☐ YELLOW
✗ BLACK

27

▲ BLACK
✗ RED
☐ GREEN
• WHITE

ACTUAL SIZE 7⅜" × 7½"

INTRIGUED as they were by nature, the Minoans would often paint the plants and flowers around them. This highly stylized version of flowering olive branches, executed in the original colors, is an impressionistic, almost dreamlike rendering of one of the dietary staples.

This fragment of nature is part of a larger bull-grappling scene, a perhaps mythological aspect of Minoan life and yet one that, because of its many depictions in paintings, sculpture, and on seals, we are forced, almost against our better judgment, to believe in.

The branches are shown bending in the wind and, as they are blown, the leaves are turned over so that their silvery undersides are revealed to us. Here the Minoans painted them in white. The number of flowers along the stalk is reduced to one, just at the end—a poorer harvest in reality, perhaps, but an easier painting to understand. Who is to say that black leaves cannot cast red shadows, as they appear here; the slim leaves with their white veins clearly delineated are echoed in red with veins unseen. And behind all, the color of the fruit, of fertility, of promise.

CIRCULAR PATTERNS were relatively rare in Crete, for the Minoans preferred forms that were infinitely expandable. This design was found on a gold medallion less than two inches in diameter. It is believed to have been a funerary ornament that was buried with the corpse. The abstract shapes, incised or cut into the medallion in a minute double line, have been adapted here into a two-color pattern for better visibility. The unbroken line that twists and curves and finally returns to its starting place may perhaps be taken as a metaphor for life itself.

ACTUAL SIZE 6⅜″ × 6¼″

THE ARGONAUT is a sea creature related to the squid and the octopus. It, too, has eight arms, but two of these are slightly larger than the others and clasp the shell, while six are free to dangle. The female, which may be up to fifteen times larger than the male, secretes a beautifully fluted shell from two of her tentacles (an unusual phenomenon in a cephalopod) in which she carries and hatches her eggs. The argonaut is usually found near the surface and moves by ejecting a jetstream of water from its body just beneath its head.

The Cretans were fascinated with this creature, which was a favorite among vase painters for hundreds of years. The curves of its shell and tentacles meshed perfectly with the Minoan predilection for the spiral, and artists stylized the argonaut's fluid physical features in many ways. In this case, the number of tentacles has been reduced to two, each containing a tightly wound spiral, as does the head. In the original vase painting, the argonaut was colored black or dark gray against a light background; the blue and white of the pattern are a modification.

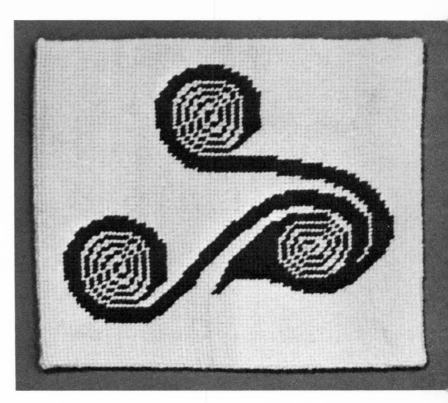

ACTUAL SIZE 7⅜" × 6½"

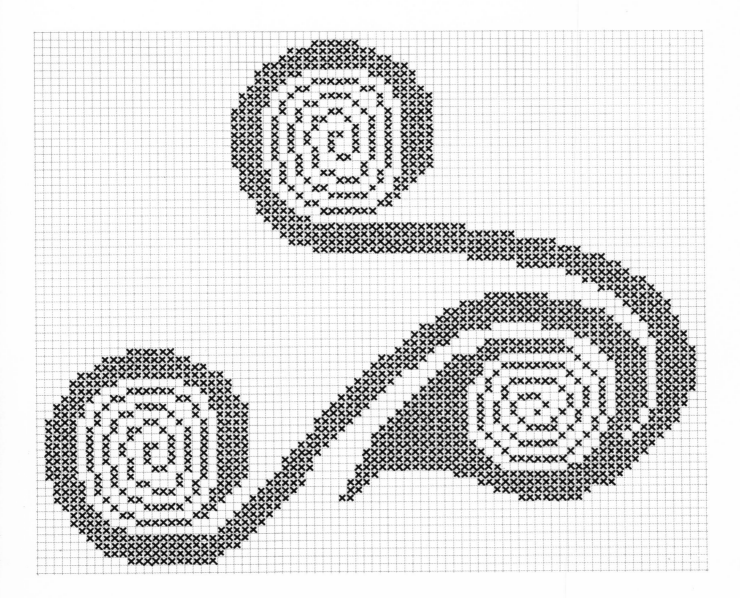

31

II DESIGNS FROM THE ART OF ANCIENT EGYPT

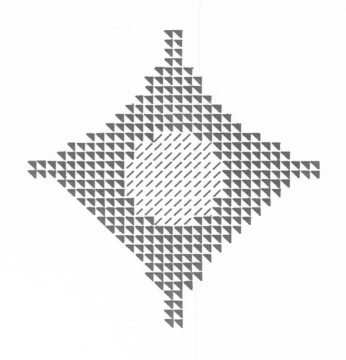

THE KINGDOM OF EGYPT lasted for three thousand years, a span more enduring than that of any nation in recorded history. From about 3200 B.C., when King Narmer united Upper and Lower Egypt, until 30 B.C., when the Roman occupation began, Egypt endured, and except for two periods five hundred years apart, when the kingdom was torn asunder by invaders, the people along the Nile remained a social and political entity of remarkable stability. The great river itself, with its periodic, predictable inundations, contributed to the continuity of the kingdom, producing a long, fertile oasis in the midst of vast deserts that insulated Egypt from its neighbors. It is not surprising, then, that the art of the ancient Egyptians should reflect the history of the country: static, monumental, slow to change. The great pyramids of Cheops and Chephren, the kings' own mausoleums, are infused with the artistic spirit of ancient Egypt. They have endured for 4,500 years as a testament to the kingdom and all it embodied.

As the kingdom persisted, so did its gods. The Egyptians had a complex mythology that remained largely intact throughout the millennia. Though various priesthoods might interpret the legends differently and shift the emphasis from one deity to another, the pantheon survived. There was, so far as we know, only one religious revolution during the centuries, and that one—led by King Akhnaton, who with his wife, the beautiful Nefertiti, substituted the splendor of one god, Aton the sun disk, for the manifold attributes of all the others—lasted less than a generation. Shortly after Akhnaton's death, however, the name of Aton was all but forgotten, and the luxurious capital that he had established at Amarna was gradually abandoned by the priests and religious functionaries.

Although there were no longer pyramid builders after the twenty-fifth century B.C., the Egyptians did not falter in their belief in an afterlife and continued to build elaborate tombs resembling underground apartments to house their spirits after death. This spirit, called the *ka*, was believed to require all the daily appurtenances of its owner after his death, and so Egyptian kings, queens, and nobility were buried in their tombs with their jewelry, furniture, and all their personal effects. A young prince's tomb would contain his toys; a princess's, her mirror and ointment jars. Many of the tombs were richly decorated, painted with designs and even scenes of daily life, so that the *ka* would presumably sense familiar surroundings while in residence. Many of the designs in this chapter have been adapted from such tomb paintings.

Much of Egyptian art is highly symbolic. For example, the combination of a papyrus flower and palmette, while lovely in itself, represents the union of Upper and Lower Egypt and was first used in this context around 3000 B.C. The king might be depicted symbolically—in the form, say, of a griffin. The deities themselves were frequently portrayed by symbols: the god Horus was a hawk; the goddess Hathor, a cow; Anubis was the jackal deity; and Nekhbet, the vulture goddess.

Most of the art of ancient Egypt has a distinctly cubelike quality, particularly apparent in the sculpture. Statues were carved as if they were meant to be seen only from the front or side: the viewer was not invited to make a circuit around an Egyptian statue, so the sculpture presents only frontal or profile views. As if to accentuate this tendency, the artists seem to have cut away very little from the original blocks. Nor did they attempt to penetrate the surface deeply but, rather, carved the figures as if to conform to the shape of the stone. Egyptian figures appear stolid and impassive perhaps because they are so blocklike; very much at rest, without a sense of motion or tension about them, they seem to exist in a state of suspended animation.

The convention of permitting only frontal or profile views extends to Egyptian painting and reliefs as well. Human figures were usually portrayed with profile heads, frontal torsos, and profile legs and feet. Occasionally this blend resulted in postures almost impossible for human beings, even triple-jointed ones, to achieve, but the Egyptians were not interested in depicting literal truth in their art. They sought to represent not what a particular scene *was* but what it should have been. For, it must be remembered, most of what has survived for us to examine is the art of the tomb—art for the *ka,* not for human eyes. And so as these figures labor, their muscles do not bulge and they do not sweat. Old age may be depicted, but physical peculiarities are seldom defined. The Egyptian ideal was the normal adult figure; even infants are small-sized adults, and rarely, except in the Amarna period (ca. 1375–1355 B.C.), was there individualized portraiture. Egyptian figures call to mind emotionless puppets that perform as ordered but with neither enthusiasm nor resentment. Only animals were permitted to break through the standard conventions. An animal—a dead lion in a hunting scene, for example—may be seen in three-quarter view; a

cow may express tension and emotion as it thrusts its head forward and sticks out its tongue from the pain of calving. The texture of a bird's downy breast was painted by the Egyptian artist, but he seldom rendered the tender touch of a loving hand.

Just as Egyptian customs and values endured over the ages, so did many of the artistic designs. There was scant need to innovate; what had sufficed for forty generations would continue to suffice, and, in fact, artists frequently used ideas that were as much as two thousand years old. Occasionally, of course, new motifs like the Minoan spiral were incorporated into their work, especially after trade with other Mediterranean and Near Eastern countries increased. The artistic exchange worked both ways: few artists in adjacent lands failed to be influenced by Egyptian designs once they were exposed to them. But those Canaanites, Phoenicians, and North Syrians never succeeded in mastering Egyptian artistry. It was only the people of the Nile—living along its fertile banks, protected by the deserts that lay beyond, and incubated by centuries of political stability—who were able to execute the exquisite art work of the Pharaohs.

ACTUAL SIZE 4⅞" × 7⅜"

THE WOVEN MAT was a common feature of Egyptian interiors. Used along walls and on ceilings to help support roofs of wood and mud, such mats, made of woven leaves and straw, were the source of the design shown here. Apparently a three-way weave was used, for in this design, the most ancient in this section, the lines seem to flow in three directions: opposing diagonals and a horizontal. If this pattern seems reminiscent of those used by southern Africans or American Indians, it may be that both of these groups, like the Egyptians, were also inspired in their art to interpret the homely, everyday objects around them. This pattern dates from approximately 2400 B.C. and originally decorated a tomb interior. The colors are close to the original.

A combination of bargello and continental stitches is used here. As in all such patterns using both stitches, in order to cover the canvas completely it is necessary to have two stitches enter the same opening in the canvas, as the chart indicates, or to have a continental stitch fall under the bargello. Where this occurs, lift the bargello stitch slightly so that the smaller stitch can slide in beneath it. Since the effect of weaving is what is desired, do the bargello first and follow with the smaller stitches.

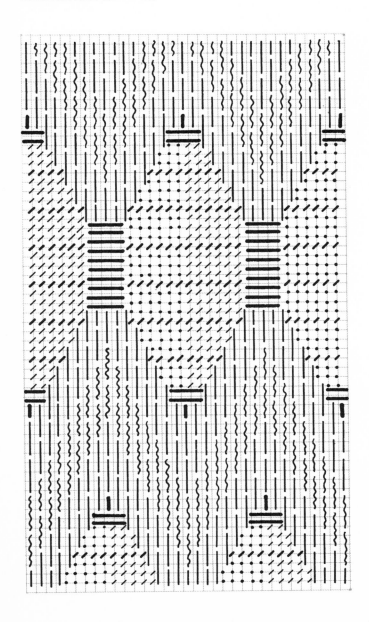

| BLACK
| WHITE
} BRICK

╱ BRICK
╱ GREEN
• YELLOW

ACTUAL SIZE 4⅞" × 3⅞"

THIS VERY SIMPLE, yet effective design, executed around 1900 B.C., is from a tomb painting originally used around the base of the walls in a kind of imitation of paneling. The motif formed a waist-high dado. Though the Egyptians used the colors shown here, this design is equally effective if only one color, in light and dark shades, is used.

Bargello stitches covering four threads are used, and the mitered corners (indicated on the chart) add a neat effect that might be lost otherwise. Because of the bargello stitches, the design can be worked very rapidly.

WHITE

RED

BLUE

BASED ON A TOMB PAINTING of about 1450 B.C., the intriguing deep red design, a background to the light blue shell-like shape, becomes a foreground motif as it swings around—a kind of snakehead. There are several such Egyptian designs with a pronounced number-nine quality that were, presumably, derived from plant forms, as were so many other Egyptian motifs. The colors used here are close to the original.

ACTUAL SIZE 8⅝" × 6"

☐ PINK
╱ YELLOW
✕ LIGHT BLUE
— GREEN
• WHITE
◣ RED

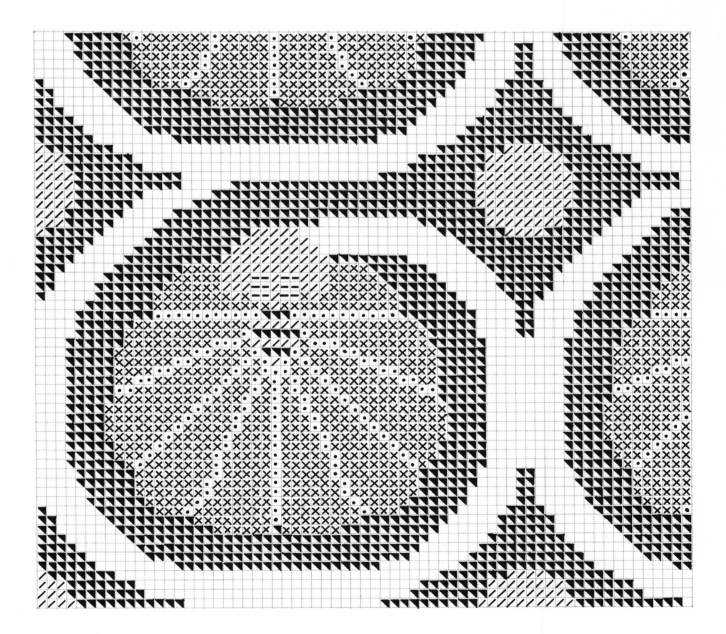

ACTUAL SIZE 13⅞" × 10½"

BASED ON A MAGNIFICENT PECTORAL, or pendant on a necklace, of King Sesostris III, now in the Cairo Museum, this pattern reveals the exquisite work of which the Egyptian jewelers were capable as early as 1800 B.C. It was made of gold with inlays of carnelian, turquoise, and lapis lazuli—semiprecious stones frequently used in ancient jewelry. That the Egyptians had a love of symmetry is evident here in their use of the same motif twice, apparently for balance. A roofed, shrinelike enclosure is seen with side walls made of lotus flowers. Nekhbet, the vulture goddess, surmounts the scene, spreading her protective wings to shield the king from evil. Under her, the king, shown twice in the form of a somewhat tubular griffin (a mythological creature with an eagle's head and a lion's body), tramples on his enemies as they beg for mercy. Inside the cartouche, or oval frame, is the name of the king, abbreviated slightly here, in hieroglyphs.

Though the gold outlines will require considerable attention, the design is easy to fill in with color once the gold is completed. Metallic yarn was used in this example, but a gold-color woolen yarn may be substituted with equal effectiveness, for unless one is extremely patient, the metallic yarn ravels easily and can be quite a nuisance to work with.

✕ BLUE

▶ GOLD

＼ TURQUOISE

• RED

☐ BLACK

CENTER

39

ACTUAL SIZE 9¼" × 6"

REPRESENTATIONS OF ANIMALS in Egyptian tombs, unless linked to specific deities, are thought by scholars to be purely decorative. This design is described as a goose, although with its solid-color, rather menacing head, it appears to be a bird that is somehow more malevolent. The pastel colors are close to those in the original painting, executed around 1450 B.C. Because one identical bird follows another so closely, it seems reasonable to speculate that a kind of stencil might have been used to make the painting. Presumably, though, the stencil technique was unknown to Egyptian artists of that time.

- • GOLD
- ✕ RED
- ╱ BLUE
- ☐ WHITE

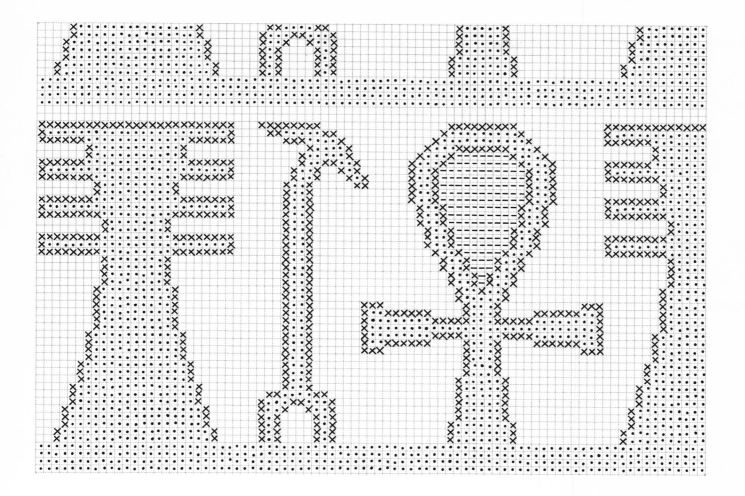

☐ BLUE
− WHITE
• BEIGE
✕ BROWN

THE *ANKH* (second from right) was the Egyptian symbol for life and has been widely reproduced. In the king's tomb from which this design, executed about 1450 B.C., was taken, two other symbols were used in connection with the *ankh*. These are the *dad* (left), symbolizing stability, and the *uas* (second from left), the bent stick usually held by the king as the symbol of his power. The *dad*, with its four projections on a sturdy, thick base, represents a row of columns, presumably with projecting capitals. These three symbols were repeated in a single row, indicating the virtues embodied in the person of the king: stability, power, and life. Although the colors used here are the same as those found in two tombs from the period, in a third tomb the symbols were painted in green against a white background, without the third color as an outline.

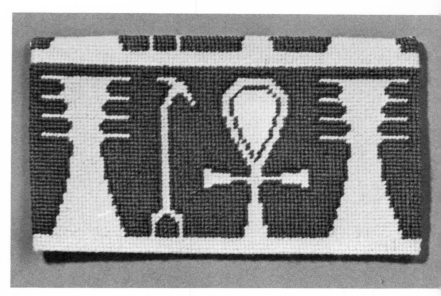

ACTUAL SIZE 7⅜" × 4¼"

THE FLOWERS OF EGYPT, the palmette, the lotus, and the papyrus, were used throughout the country's history as decorative motifs. This highly stylized palmette, even in the rather sedate color combination used by the Egyptians, has an almost Art Deco quality about it. Like other Egyptian designs in this section, the palmette was one of a band of identical flowers, as indicated in the needlepoint sample. It was adapted from a coffin cover painted about 700 B.C.

ACTUAL SIZE 6½" × 3½"

CENTER
STITCH

∠ BLACK
✕ BRICK
• LIME
☐ GOLD

HATHOR, goddess of love and joy and feeder of the dead, was represented in both human form and animal form (as a cow). As a human, Hathor was always seen with her cow's ears—for easy identification, we must assume. This depiction, one of a series of such Hathor heads, formed a frieze, or ornamental band, around the tops of the walls of a tomb painted about 1450 B.C. The frieze terminated at the end of the goddess's neck, and just below it ran a series of colored rectangles that served to separate the band from the large wall painting below. The capital-like shape of the crown worn by the goddess, as well as the placement of the heads at the uppermost portion of the walls, gives the head a columnar quality; the series formed a kind of wall of painted supports for the roof. Such walls of columns were a common feature of Egyptian architecture.

The colors employed here are those used by the Egyptian artists. Women's faces were usually yellow, while men were painted a dark red. The darker strands in the wig are a needlepoint adaptation of the darker brushstrokes used by the artists to give texture to the hair. Egyptian women used many cosmetics, judging from the jars of ointments and unguents found in large numbers in their tombs. The green around Hathor's eyes indicates the powdered malachite, a copper ore green or blue in color, that was ground on small palettes and mixed with oil for outlining the eyes of both men and women.

To duplicate the original painting, this design should be reproduced as a series of heads with perhaps five stitches separating them.

ACTUAL SIZE 6½" × 7⅞"

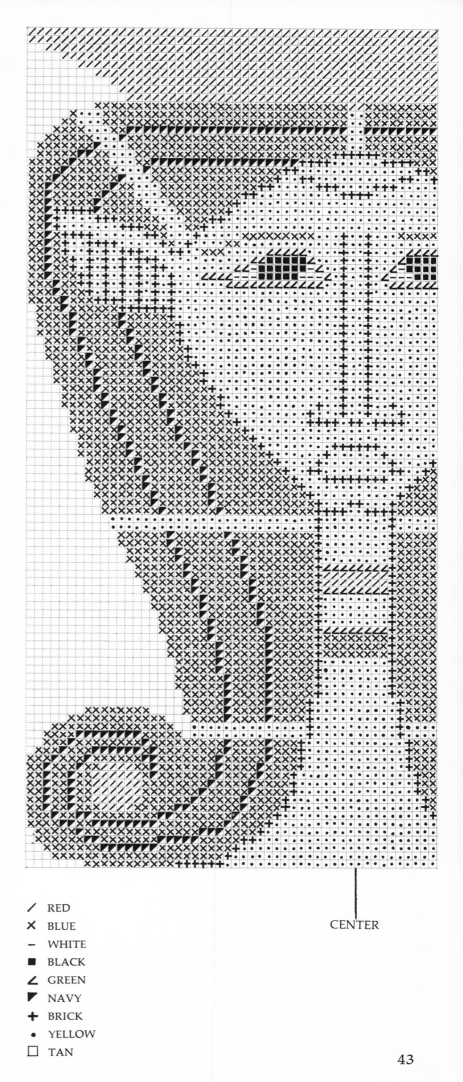

CENTER

/ RED
X BLUE
– WHITE
■ BLACK
∠ GREEN
◣ NAVY
+ BRICK
• YELLOW
□ TAN

43

□ NAVY
− WHITE
◤ RED
✕ BLUE
╲ GREEN
• YELLOW

ACTUAL SIZE 8½″ × 11⅝″

THE MOTIF of papyrus and palmette was almost two thousand years old when it was painted on the harem wall in the palace of Rameses III in about 1150 B.C. The bright colors of the alternating green and blue stems against the deep blue-gray background are highlighted by the use of red, yellow, and white. This design, like many of the others in the collection, can be continued horizontally or vertically to fill any size canvas.

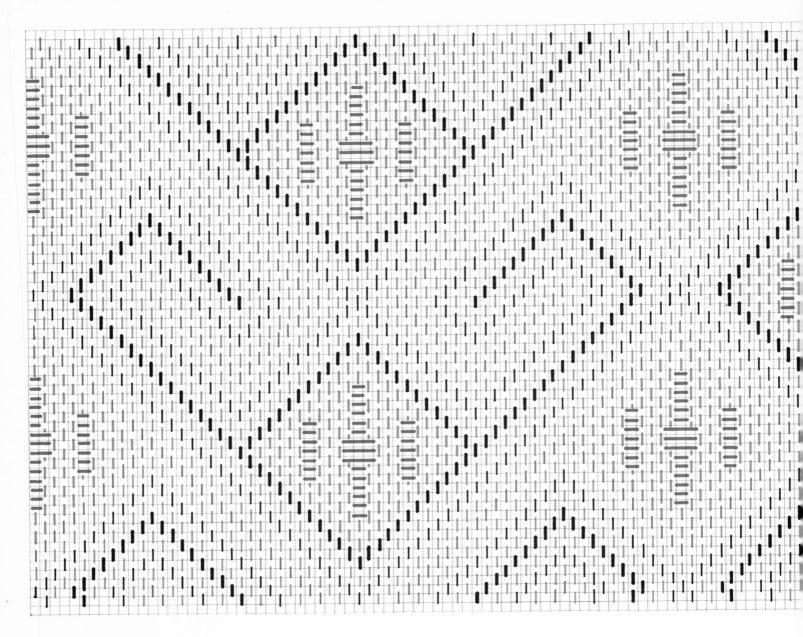

| | LIGHT BROWN
| | DARK BROWN
| | LIGHT BLUE
| | NAVY BLUE
| | WHITE
| | PINK

THIS DESIGN, from a tomb ceiling of about 600 B.C., was derived from a tomb-painting design thirteen hundred years older. Though the later painting was rendered in the colors used here instead of the original blue and black, the two almost identical designs indicate how content the Egyptians were to reuse the motifs of their past.

The pattern is a winding one that turns corners many times and might be difficult to follow for the inexperienced needleworker. Most of the bargello stitches cover only two threads of the canvas. An important point to remember is that the blue- and brown-outlined diamonds do not line up exactly even on the canvas—there is a two-thread difference between them.

Inside the lozenges, bargello stitches covering four threads are used for part of the central dark blue forms. If desired, they can be omitted for simplicity's sake. Here as elsewhere, two stitches will occasionally fall into the same opening in the canvas, as indicated in the chart, and one must be careful in their placement. Also, there are tiny filling stitches covering only one thread of the canvas that should be used to help straighten the outlines of the shapes within the diamonds. All this may sound more complicated than working the design should be, for it is a repetition of symmetrical motifs. After one repeat is finished, subsequent ones will be easy. Writing down the number of stitches in a line of any single color will prove quite helpful.

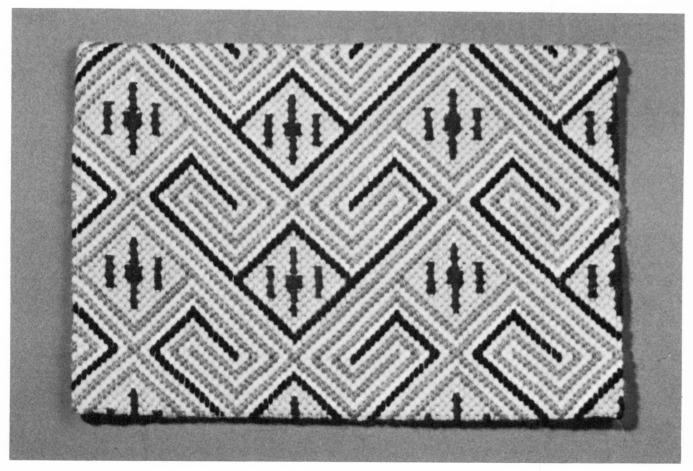

ACTUAL SIZE 8" × 5¾"

III DESIGNS FROM THE ART OF THE ANCIENT NEAR EAST

IN THE EIGHTH MILLENNIUM B.C., it is now generally believed, cavemen in the highlands began filtering down into the fertile area between Palestine and the Zagros Mountains northwest of the Persian Gulf. Nomadic hunters and gatherers of wild-growing grains, they congregated in this land around the Tigris and Euphrates rivers, the seedbed of Western civilization. Here they learned to cultivate crops, to conserve them for survival through fallow seasons, to clothe themselves and build shelters. Once the benefits of communal efforts became apparent, village life was born.

On the arid Tigris-Euphrates plain, village settlements were separated by vast desert stretches. Dams and canals for drainage and irrigation were developed early, which eased but never wholly contained the rampaging spring floods. In Mesopotamia, men lived in fear of the savage and unpredictable floods—and in even greater fear of the gods who they believed caused them.

Almost all of the early art of Mesopotamia is concerned in some way with religious belief. Most images are of deities or demons or sacred symbols, and even when a mortal—the king himself, for example—was depicted, he was posed entreating or confronting the gods. Little of early Mesopotamian art was purely decorative, with the exception perhaps of painted pottery, an art that ceased soon after technology had sufficiently advanced so that the finest vessels were constructed of stone or metal.

The principal landmark in each ancient Mesopotamian town, the temple of the local deity, was likely to have consumed hundreds of thousands of man-hours in its construction, since the basic building material was the hand-made mud brick. The temple was built on a high, man-made platform that symbolized the mountaintop dwelling of the god. One such platform, the remains of which survived for 3,000 years at Warka, the Biblical Erech, was composed of compressed clay and millions of mud bricks, rose forty feet above the plain, and covered an entire acre. The mountain, when rendered by Mesopotamian artists as a hill or triangle covered by a scale pattern, was thus a shrinelike symbol. Water, too, was of holy significance, for its absence or abundance suggested how acceptable the deities found the service of their worshipers. Many images of gods and goddesses holding vases overflowing with water were worked in sculpture in the round and brick reliefs; the fate of the crops and therefore of the people themselves was shown to be literally in the hands of the gods.

Prominent among the widely used methods of conveying religious concepts in the ancient Near East was the cylinder seal, an object about the size of a man's thumb, occasionally made of semiprecious stones and engraved with designs on the exterior surface that were readily reproduced when rolled over wet clay or any other receptive material. When a vessel was to be sealed with clay or a package tied with cord, the knot would be covered with a layer of wet clay and the seal rolled over it—primarily, it is thought, to impart the religious or magical efficacy contained in the engraving to the contents of the parcel or vessel; the safety of the package was secondary. The problem of creating appropriate designs for a surface that might be only partially seen (when, for example, only a portion of the seal was rolled over wet clay) or repeated (where the clay surface was wide enough for the seal to be turned twice or three times around its circumference) was solved early in the history of Mesopotamian art. The scenes depicted on cylinder seals were to influence Near Eastern artists profoundly for millennia, for the formulas were scarcely varied.

Near Eastern mythological subjects are revealed constantly in the seals. Though some scenes are readily understood narratives (e.g., lions attacking the flocks), most are religious depictions, only some of which are understood by scholars. Animals might fight in a great mêlée and bull-headed men, fire-breathing dragons, and monstrous forms of all sorts confront one another in attempts to commit grave injury. The seal motifs of copulating serpents and beasts whose long necks interlace about each other have been interpreted as aspects of the underground god of natural vitality from whom all life springs. Also seen occasionally was the lion-headed eagle, symbol of the rain god, and, more frequently, herbivorous animals and plants, thought to represent the Great Mother. In heraldic arrangements of animals, very common on cylinder seals, the animals are seen confronting each other, and when the seal was rolled around its circumference more than once, the animals became addorsed, or back to back, an equally symmetrical heraldic arrangement.

From about the third millennium B.C., the history of the Tigris-Euphrates region is a story of successive waves of immigrants and how they were assimilated into the prevailing culture. A vast, open area at the center of civilization in western Asia, the "fertile crescent" lay open to marauders and peaceable peoples alike, each infusing the art of the region with new motifs that were adapted and perpetuated. Though city-states were isolated, their religious beliefs, and thus the overall patterns of culture, were similar. Cooperation among the settlements, furthermore, was a necessity in order to maintain the irrigation system. Periods of relative peace were often abruptly ended as a new group of invaders attacked Mesopotamian settlements. Political stability eventually returned, along with the older forms of art and culture, as temples were rebuilt. Inevitably, enrichment occurred in the process; the Kassites, for example, introduced a new art medium to Mesopotamia—the use of molded brick—that reached fruition in Babylon a thousand years later. Two motifs that entered Mesopotamian art as a result of the political turmoil, the sacred tree (or tree of life, a plantlike form that was elaborately stylized) and the crested griffin, blended with traditional images: vegetable motifs had long been used as symbols of the gods, and unnatural creatures and demons had been depicted in sculpture and on cylinder seals for centuries.

The people we now call the Assyrians gradually assumed dominance in northern Mesopotamia in the centuries after the foreign incursions. Assyria to the north and Babylon to the south faced invasions of outsiders periodically and, thus weakened, formed alliances either with or against one another depending on the compatibility of the rulers involved. By the early ninth century B.C., after confronting steady pressure from peoples to the west for centuries, the Assyrians began to behave in the manner now re-garded as characteristic of them throughout their history: they conquered every foe within their orbit.

The art of the Assyrians appears more secular and narrative than that of earlier Mesopotamians. Assyrian deities are not seen; the king confronts only their symbols. The Assyrians preferred to decorate their palaces with relief sculpture implying the vast power of the king. Winged human-headed bulls called *Lamassu*, carved in stone relief, guarded the throne room of Sargon's palace at Khorsabad, while a panel of glazed bricks, depicting fierce animals and religious symbols, protected his temple. Subsequent kings decorated their palaces with stone relief sculptures, narrating the events of their victorious battles in vivid and bloodthirsty detail. Kings are also seen participating in lion hunts, rituals that are thought by some scholars to have a religious connotation. While the intent of the sculpture is to glorify the king, it is clear that the animals engaged the sympathy of Assyrian artists; as the king's antagonists they are powerfully rendered but, wounded and dying, are almost tenderly depicted.

The glory of the Assyrian kings vanished when their capital at Nineveh fell in 612 B.C. to the Babylonian general Nebuchadnezzar, who, upon ascending the throne, built his great palace in Babylon and began to restore war-ravaged temples throughout Babylonia as well. The art produced by the Babylonians for their temples in this period mixed Assyrian elements with the older, more traditional southern Mesopotamian motifs. As an indication of the nature of Babylonian art, the principal decorations of Nebuchadnezzar's throne room were not the Assyrians' fierce war memorials but colored, molded-brick flowers and columns.

The extensive temple building resulted in part from the cultural upheaval caused by the presence of the religiously sophisticated Medes and Jews in Babylonia. Ancient polytheism and the rituals it engendered began to appear frail and naïve to the Babylonians as Nebuchadnezzar hoped to counter the ferment by rekindling interest in the old gods. He was too late. Events in the Near East were moving with rapidity. Cyrus, king of the Medes and Persians, had gained a reputation in Babylonia for treating the peoples he had conquered with justice and kindness. As he and his armies approached, he created a fifth column within Babylonia itself. In 539 B.C. Cyrus overcame the Babylonians, and Mesopotamia, where civilization had begun, became a provincial outpost, its harsh strength vitiated, no longer able to direct its own destiny, worship its old gods, or create its own images.

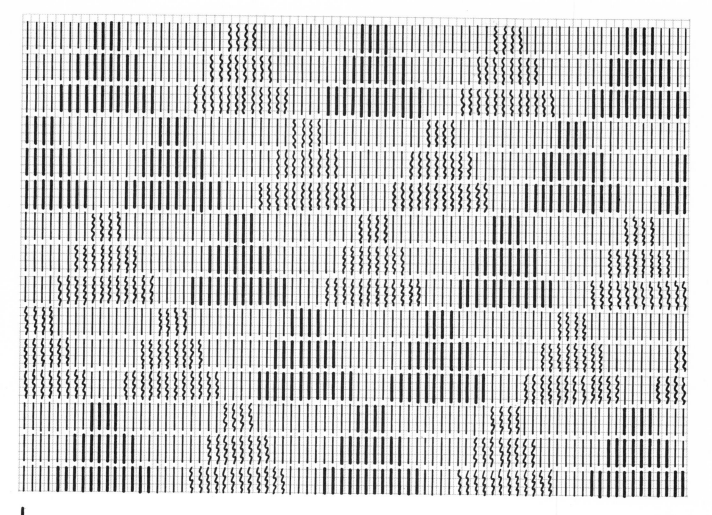

| BLACK

| TAN

{ RED

THIS BARGELLO DESIGN is derived from a supporting column in an ancient temple erected in the second half of the fourth millennium B.C. at Warka near the Euphrates River. One of a series of similarly patterned columns each measuring nine feet in diameter (the height of the columns is uncertain), it was covered with a weatherproof coating of thousands of four-inch-long baked-clay cones that were dipped in red, black and buff pigment, inserted into the mud plaster sheathing the columns, and arranged to form a series of geometric patterns.

In this adaptation, each group of four bargello stitches represents one of the clay cones. The pattern resulted as the cones were grouped in sets of six and combined to form series of ascending and descending triangles. The pattern can be worked very rapidly once the first series of triangles is established. The red and black triangles always have their points uppermost, while the beige acts as a buffer, separating the two, and is always stitched with its point toward the bottom of the canvas.

ACTUAL SIZE 6½" × 6½"

AN INLAY OF RED JASPER, sea shell, and lapis lazuli set into bitumen on the wood sounding box of a harp was the origin of this design. Ornamented with a cast-gold, three-dimensional bull's head, the harp was found in the "royal cemetery" at Ur and dates from perhaps 2800 B.C. Only one of a number of such precious objects found at this site, it exemplifies the extraordinary work of which the Sumerians were capable.

ACTUAL SIZE 6¼" × 6⅜"

WHITE

BLUE

RED

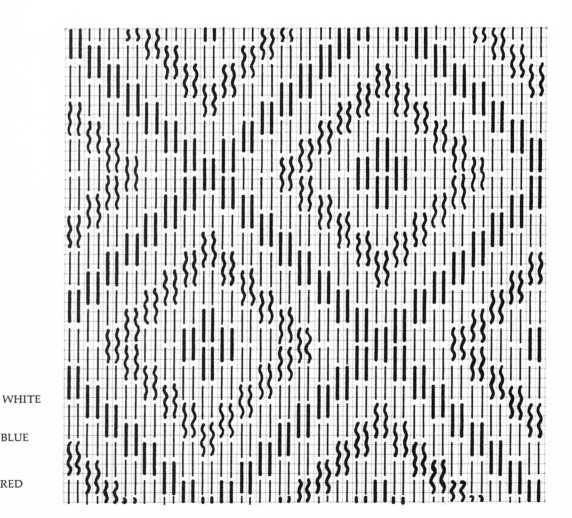

THIS WOVEN, ribbon-like pattern is a stylization of a fragment of a fresco found at the palace of King Zimrilim at Mari, on the Euphrates River. Zimrilim was a contemporary of King Hammurabi of Babylon, and the palace therefore dates to about 1750 B.C. Just above this pattern was a depiction of an ankle and foot, so it is possible that the weaving was meant to represent a rug or carpet of some sort. The original colors consisted of red and white bands against a white background.

Because both continental and bargello stitches are used in this pattern, care should be taken to make sure that the continental stitches pass under the bargello work.

ACTUAL SIZE 6⅛″ × 6¼″

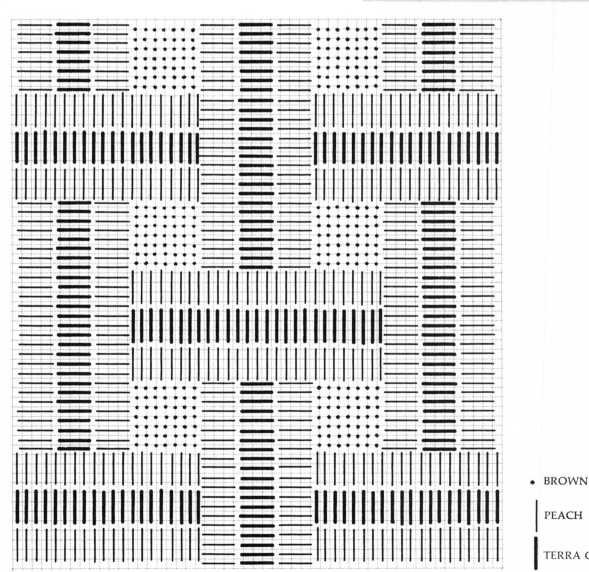

• BROWN

| PEACH

| TERRA COTTA

53

THE SYMMETRICAL ARRANGEMENT of animals was an artistic convention dating back to the beginning of ancient Near Eastern art. Confronted animals, seen frequently on cylinder seals, possess a symbolic value usually connected with religious beliefs. This scene, reconstructed from a fresco fragment at the palace at Mari, was one of many similar depictions, though the type of animals might vary considerably.

The ibex, shown here, was an animal common in the Near East and undoubtedly served as a source of food. It was probably a sacred animal, too—possibly the symbol of a deity. The other element in this scene, the mountain, composed of overlapping fish-scale-like forms, was a sacred concept to the Meso-potamians, who viewed and depicted it as hallowed ground. The belief extended, perhaps, to the ancient Hebrews as well, for Moses received the Ten Commandments at the top of Mount Sinai. The tree at the peak of the mountain is a fertility symbol and is undoubtedly rich in religious meaning.

The motif is, in short, a very old and sacred one in the Near East and should not be seen as pure design divorced from its religious significance. It has been executed here in the colors that were ascribed to it by the archaeologist who excavated Mari; of course, the exact shades of the original are impossible to duplicate.

ACTUAL SIZE 9" × 8⅞"

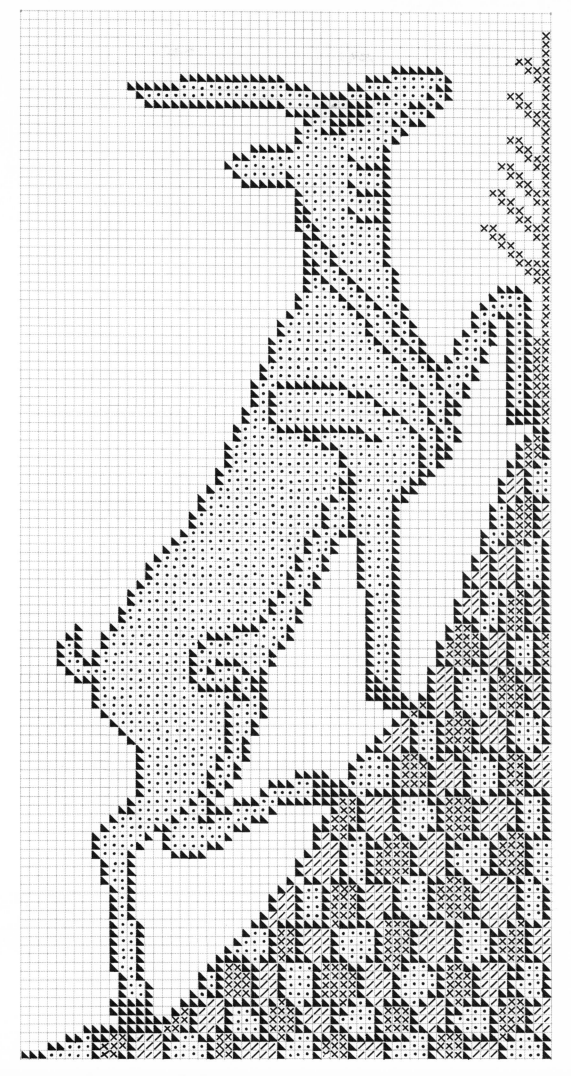

/ YELLOW
✗ GREEN
• PINK
◣ BLACK
☐ WHITE

55

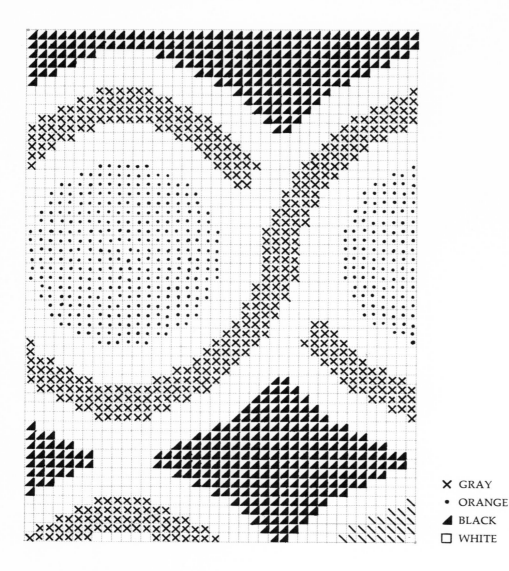

✕ GRAY
● ORANGE
◢ BLACK
☐ WHITE

THE *GUILLOCHE*, or twist, was a common motif in the ancient Near East long before the fresco (the origin of this needlepoint design) from Zimrilim's palace at Mari was painted. Variations of this simple twist were to have a long life in the history of art during succeeding millennia. It is believed that the motif is derived from the twisting of snakes, a theme that had fascinated the Mesopotamians for centuries, and survives even today in the caduceus, the staff-and-snakes symbol of the medical profession.

In the original color scheme, the lozenges between the rows of circles were a salmon pink, a shade that jars the modern eye when used in combination with orange, and the half lozenges at the edges were black.

ACTUAL SIZE 6″ × 6¾″

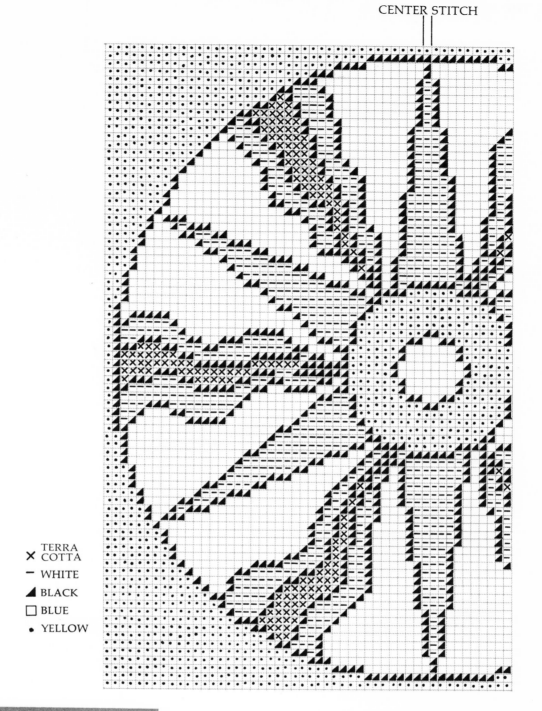

× TERRA
  COTTA
- WHITE
◢ BLACK
☐ BLUE
• YELLOW

THIS SIX-POINTED STAR with its flamelike emanations is thought to have been a solar motif, a symbol of the sun god, perhaps. Found at Mari on an offering box, presumably a container for temple treasures, it measures about twelve inches in diameter. The original coloration included only the terra cotta, white, blue and black; the yellow is an addition to a blend that seems peculiarly somber for a symbol of the sun.

ACTUAL SIZE 8⅛" × 8¼"

TOP

GOLD

BROWN

TERRA COTTA

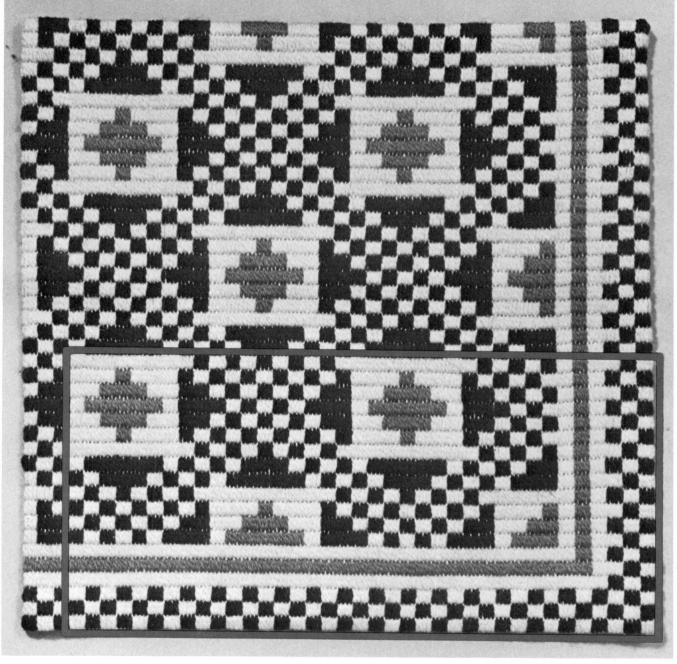

ACTUAL SIZE 11⅞" × 12"

ANOTHER UNUSUAL DISCOVERY made at Mari was the mosaic that formed the basis of this design. Originally the tesserae, or small stone pieces, were set into wood that, of course, had disintegrated by the time the mosaic was unearthed; it is clear that the excavators have done a masterful job of re-creation. The original mosaic measured just thirteen by twenty inches and contained only two shades or textures—the stones themselves and the wood background. A third color has been introduced here, but two colors might easily be used.

The diagonal rows of squares form a motif that was used extensively in American quilts of the last century and is known as a double Irish chain. One corner of the design has been illustrated, and you can use it as a mirror image to project the treatment of the other three corners. If you have difficulty picturing the "mirror image," you might find it easier to turn the chart upside down and work the other side of the design in that way. The motif can be repeated to make whatever size you want.

CENTER STITCH

ACTUAL SIZE 4½″ × 7¼″

THE SACRED TREE, or tree of life, is a motif still found in oriental rugs. The symbol, prominent in the Bible (Genesis 2:9 and 3:22; Proverbs 3:18 and 11:30), formed a major element in the cotton chintzes that were imported by the English from India in the seventeenth and eighteenth centuries. The original of this design was a carving in ivory, a precious material fit for a deity. The colors are a modern addition, and the design has been slightly modified for the sake of the scale of the needlepoint. This sacred tree was carved by the Kassites, a group who invaded Mesopotamia from the Kurdish mountains. It is dated to the second half of the second millennium B.C.

☐ PEACH
✗ GREEN
• WHITE

/ LIGHT GREEN

✕ DARK GREEN

⋏ ROYAL BLUE

◢ DARK PURPLE

• LIGHT PURPLE

✛ MEDIUM PURPLE

□ LIGHT BLUE

BARGELLO

▌ DARK PURPLE

▎ ROYAL BLUE

PATTERNED TEXTILES may well have been used as rugs in the Near East circa 800 B.C., for it is believed that this needlepoint design, derived from a marble door sill found at the Assyrian palace at Khorsabad, was itself based on a rug pattern. The lotus flower used in the border is an innovation in Mesopotamia, for the motif was unknown to the Assyrians before they invaded Egypt in the seventh century B.C. It may perhaps have been borrowed from an Egyptian object obtained through trade.

ACTUAL SIZE 6⅝" × 7⅛"

ACTUAL SIZE 9¼" × 8¼"

THE THRONE ROOM of Nebuchadnezzar's great palace in Babylon was the source of these volute and palmette forms, connected by flowers. The illustration shows only the upper third of the motif, for the shafts continue downward to make column-like forms. Made of color-glazed bricks, four of the columns formed the central panel in the wall of the room and were surrounded by bands of stylized flowers. The wall and the palace that contained it were probably executed in the latter part of Nebuchadnezzar's reign, which lasted slightly more than forty years (ca. 604–562 B.C.).

Only the upper part of the column is illustrated here; the rest of the column is rather simple in shape and merely a continuation of the shaft intersected by two more series of triple bands, until the shaft ends on a base consisting of the three bands. One can, of course, ignore the shaft of the columns and embroider only the tops of the columns and the connecting flowers—a lovely design in itself. But for those who are ambitious, the entire motif is 274 rows in height, with the top 83 rows comprising the volute and palmette capital, not including the first series of three bands. Next come the 17 rows for the three bands. The first 41 rows of the shaft follow and then 17 rows of the triple bands, and the series continues twice more: 41, 17, 41, and then the column ends with the 17 rows of the three bands of color.

On a number 14 canvas, the whole motif would measure almost twenty inches in length—a bit large, perhaps, for a pillow, but if the length of the shaft were reduced by a third (that is, the last series of 58 rows were omitted), a pillow of just over fifteen inches would result—a more comfortable length.

✕ ORANGE

• WHITE

╱ LIGHT BLUE

☐ DARK BLUE

63

IV DESIGNS FROM THE ART OF GREECE AND ROME

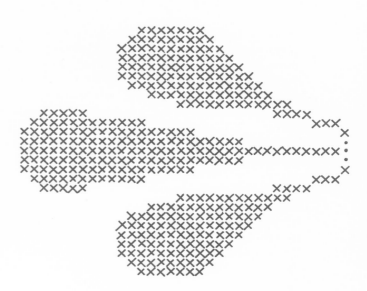

HOMER'S *Iliad* and *Odyssey*, scholars now believe, should be read not only as fictional epic poems, but also as fairly accurate accounts of life in prehistoric Greece. Tradition suggests that the poet lived in the last half of the eighth century B.C., some five hundred years after the events he chronicled supposedly occurred. The world Homer describes was that of Agamemnon, King of Mycenae and the undoubted overlord of much of Greece. Though the Mycenaeans lived for the most part in the Argolid, the southern area of the Greek mainland, they may have shared certain cultural elements with the Minoans. Like them, the Mycenaeans erected huge palaces with frescoed interiors at Tiryns, Pylos, and Mycenae but theirs were highly fortified with huge walls. The apex of their civilization came almost two centuries after that of the Minoans—in about 1300 B.C.—and like them, the Mycenaeans carried on extensive trade with Egypt and the Near East and achieved a complex society that was abruptly ended not by natural forces, as in Crete, but by invasion.

The Dorian invaders were Greeks, perhaps from Thessaly in the north, whose arrival in the Peloponnesus in about 1200 B.C. spread a cultural blackout over the land that lasted for centuries. It was not until the beginning of the eighth century B.C. that Greek society had advanced to the point that art, in the form of decorated pottery, could develop.

The earliest Greek pottery was painted in a geometric style with horizontal bands of linear, abstract designs like triangles, checkers, or circles. Many of these vases were over five feet high and were used as grave markers. Often they had holes in the bottom so that liquid offerings could be poured through to the dead below.

In the seventh century B.C., when trade with the Near East was again opened, new oriental motifs like rosettes, interlaces, palmettes, and animals both real and imaginary entered the repertory of the vase painter. The old geometric forms were executed on the foot and handles—areas of relative unimportance —and gradually one large narrative scene came to dominate the body of the vase. At first the scene consisted of painted black figures set against a terracotta ground. Then just before 500 B.C. the reverse color scheme was adopted when it was discovered that greater detail could be painted on a red figure than on a black one.

Greek pottery is a unique ceramic phenomenon. It is deliberately unglazed. Even though a glaze was available to them, Greek artists preferred the matte finish of the pots, obviously delighting in the velvety sheen. The horizontal ridges left by the potters' fingers as the ceramic pieces were thrown on the wheel can still be felt on the interior surface. A thick black pigment was applied to the outer surface with a feather or stiff-bristled brush that left a slight groove in the clay surface. Other areas were filled in with a yellow-brown wash, white, and a purplish hue. Firing the pots was a complicated process that involved considerable skill. The shape of a vase was carefully thought out, for shape was strictly dependent on function. Greek vases were not merely decorative; they were used for the storage and mixing of oil, water, wine, or perfumes. Handles had to be large enough to be grasped easily and were contoured to fit comfortably in the hand.

Much attention has been given to Greek vases because they are about the only surviving evidence of Greek painting. Presumably wall and panel paintings were also executed by Greek artists, but they have vanished, and art historians have made the assumption that vase painting did not differ markedly from the larger works except in scale. The process of constant thought and gradual redefinition that the Greeks gave to their pottery was, of course, extended to all of their aesthetic endeavors.

The Hellenes strove ceaselessly to express their

ideals in their art. The human form was almost always sculpted at the peak of its physical development—a reflection of the Greeks' delight in the youthful shapes of men and women. In their attempts to render physical perfection, they seldom chose subjects beyond the prime of life or with odd or unlovely features. Whether depicting deities or mortals, Greek sculptors created physical types rather than individuals.

With the conquests of Alexander the Great in the second half of the fourth century B.C., Greek aesthetic concepts were spread throughout a vast arc of territory southeast of Greece and fanning across Asia to the borders of India. The cross-fertilization of Greek and Asian artistic inclinations helped to produce what has become known as Hellenistic art. Old Greek forms were infused with a new reality. Violence, emotion, and pain were expressed. The sculpture of the Hellenistic era began to concern itself with individuals and their differences. Men and women were shown to have grown old and to have been moved by life's travail.

Despite the high admiration in which the Romans held Greek forms, which were copied extensively, they extended the trends developed during the Hel-

lenistic era. It was the Romans who created the portrait statue, the ultimate individualization of sculptural subject matter. The Romans dealt not in myths, as did the Greeks, in their monumental relief sculpture but in leaving a testament of real people and actual events.

The Romans were superb engineers who used a new material—concrete—to create such quotidian delights as sewers, as well as aqueducts, bridges, and magnificent temple complexes. The concrete surface was often faced with brick, small pieces of stone, or smooth plaster to render it more attractive. To enliven floor surfaces in buildings throughout the empire, mosaics composed of small pieces of stone called tesserae were created, frequently in lovely geometric patterns.

▲▲

Few examples of Roman painting have survived other than those buried in Pompeii and Herculaneum by the eruption of Mount Vesuvius in A.D. 79. Most Pompeiian paintings were large-scale murals with prominent architectural or landscape elements. Sacred rites were the subject of one series. Aside from a few scattered works, the development of Roman painting is, sadly, almost unknown to present-day scholars.

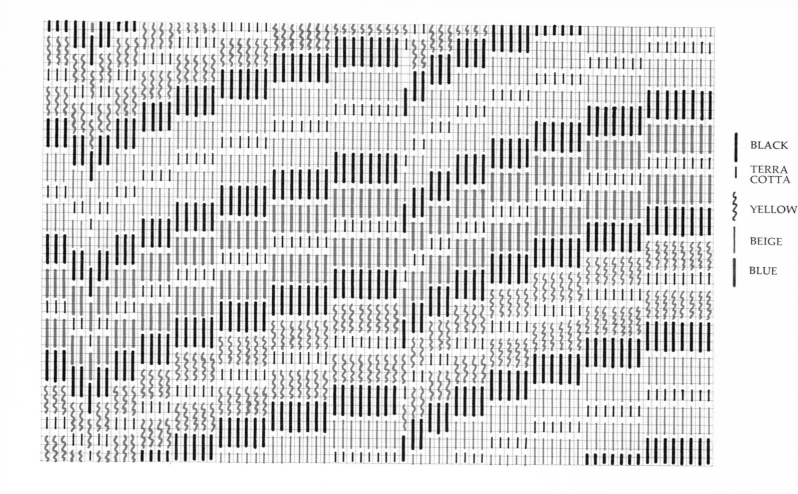

	BLACK
	TERRA COTTA
	YELLOW
	BEIGE
	BLUE

HEINRICH SCHLIEMANN was the nineteenth-century German amateur archaeologist who was convinced of the historical authenticity of Homer. Steadfast in his belief, he unearthed many sites mentioned in the texts of the Homeric epics, among them Troy, Mycenae, and the palace fortress of Tiryns. The fresco fragment from which this design was adapted was part of a large scene at Tiryns that Schliemann thought depicted a winged animal. The upward rhythm of the lines evoked, for him, layers of feathers lying atop one another.

What Schliemann actually saw was one half of this design. It has been doubled here for the sake of symmetry and balance. The ever-ascending lines convey the impression of a bird in flight.

ACTUAL SIZE 10¾″ × 5½″

ACTUAL SIZE 8" × 6¾"

THIS NEEDLEPOINT DESIGN is based on a rosette-band fresco that was painted freehand, according to Schliemann, for no two rosettes are exactly alike. The colors are very close to the original as depicted in Schliemann's book *Tiryns,* published in the United States in 1885. The excavator described this particular fragment as being part of the decoration of the women's hall in the palace; it is dated to around the thirteenth century B.C. The irregularity of the border has been adjusted slightly, since the original had no continuity of pattern.

In this design, contrary to others where a combination of continental and bargello stitches is used, it is easier to do the continental stitches first so that the bargello stitches will lie over them.

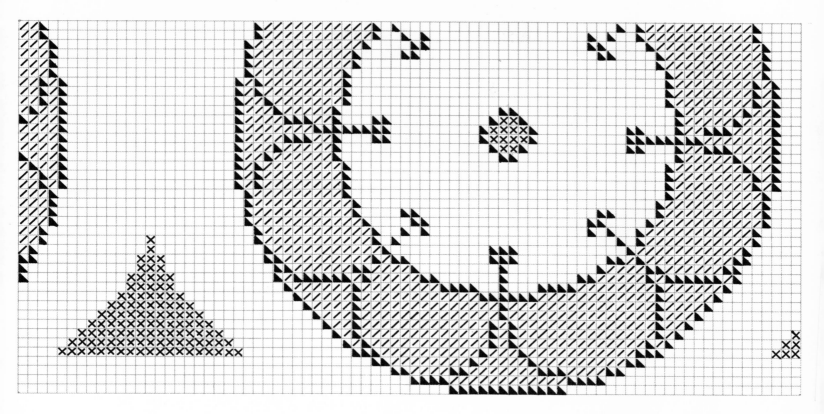

□ BEIGE
✕ TERRA COTTA
╱ BLUE
◣ BLACK

BORDER DETAIL

⟨ LIGHT ORANGE

⟨ TERRA COTTA

| BLUE

▮ BLACK

ACTUAL SIZE 7½" × 10⅜"

IN THE VOCABULARY of art history, a single line that forms a series of angles as it goes this way and that is called a meander, supposedly after a river in Phrygia that made tortuous twists and curves. Two meanders are shown here; the simpler one is often referred to as a Greek key. The designs were found on a geometric-style vase that dates from the eighth century B.C. The pale orange shade is an addition, for the original colors were simply terra cotta and black, with the meander itself painted in a dilution of the black pigment.

This design is far easier to do if the black continental stitches are executed first, for they serve as the outline for the rest.

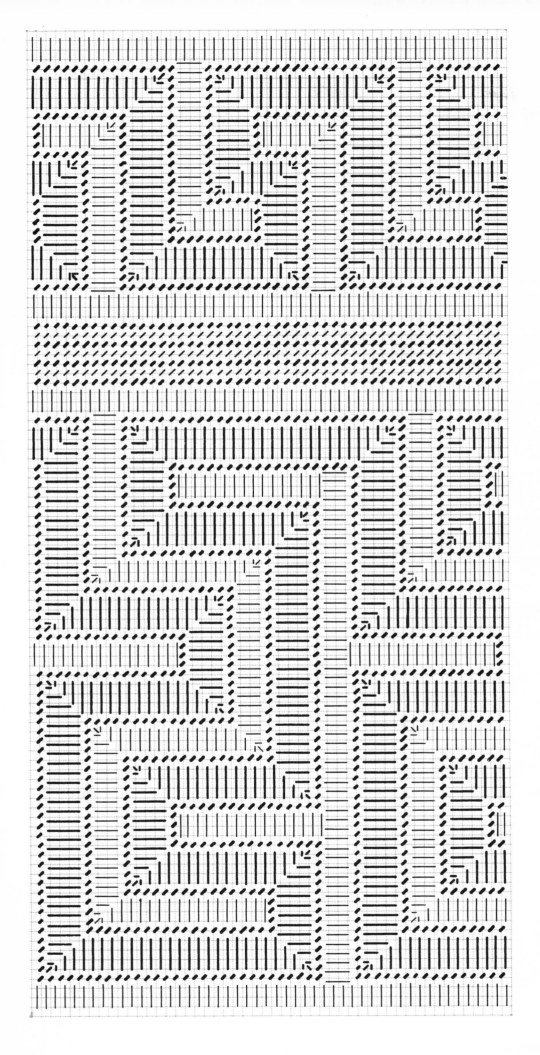

	TERRA COTTA
	PEACH
●	BLACK
/	TERRA COTTA

71

THE INTERLACE, or *guilloche*, is an oriental motif that entered Greek art with the onset of trade with the Near East. This design, dated from the last quarter of the seventh century B.C., is derived from a border on a chalice made on the island of Chios, just off the coast of Anatolia. The central portion of the pot contains a row of horned animals, along with birds and a spiral design—all motifs previously unknown in Greek art. The colors reproduced here are very close to the original.

Although only one end of the design is charted, one can replicate the other end simply by turning the chart upside down, for the design is continuous in both directions.

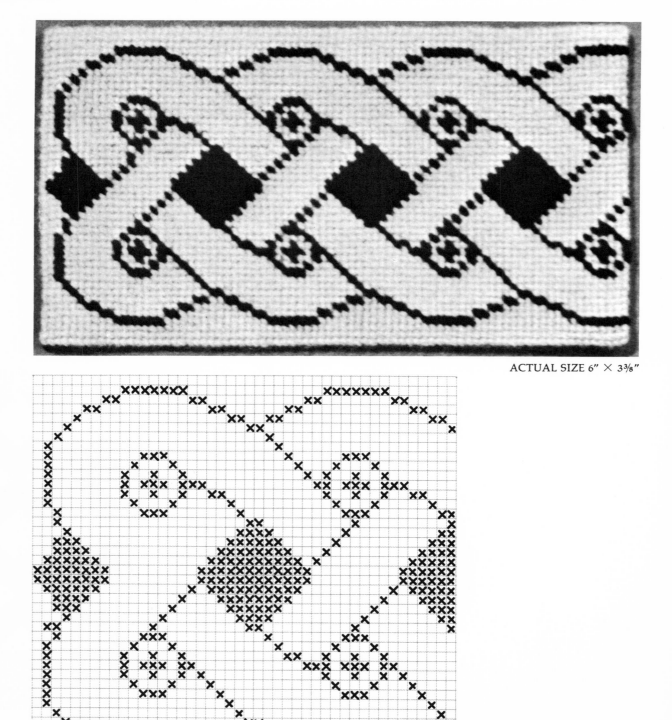

ACTUAL SIZE 6" × 3⅜"

THE ERUPTION of Mount Vesuvius preserved many Roman treasures for modern eyes, among them this *trompe l'oeil* floor mosaic from the *cella*, or inner room, of the Temple of Apollo at Pompeii. Composed of small lozenge shapes of green-and-white marble and slate, the pavement must have thrown many Romans off-balance because of the strange visual sensation produced by the pattern. Yet similar kinds of floors were laid throughout the Roman Empire, from Antioch in Syria to Tunisia in North Africa. Among nineteenth-century American quilters, the pattern was known as baby's blocks and can be seen in many variations and media today. The bargello stitches are easy to do, and because the scale is small, there should be few problems encountered with snags or pulls.

LIGHT BROWN

DARK BROWN

BEIGE

ACTUAL SIZE 4½″ × 3½″

THE NAMES of ancient artists are for the most part unknown. The vase, however, on which this design appears was signed by Exekias, one of the finest Greek vase painters. Executed about 530 B.C., the design was painted on the neck of a pear-shaped vase called an amphora, used for the storage of wine. It consists of a double lotus flower and a series of palmettes attached to a chain. The use of the third color, a purple shade, is not at all unusual in Greek pottery, but it tended to wear off the surface easily and so cannot always be seen.

ACTUAL SIZE 5" × 7½"

☐ TERRA COTTA
• PURPLE
✗ BLACK

A KRATER was a large bowl often used for mixing wine and water, for the Greeks diluted their wine with at least two parts water. The particular krater from which this palmette design was adapted was recently acquired by the Metropolitan Museum of Art in New York under curious and controversial circumstances and at the cost of a small fortune. It was painted by Euphronios, probably during the last quarter of the sixth century B.C. The palmette was a motif derived from the Near East, perhaps related to the sacred tree, and often used as a border on vases, both red- and black-figured.

ACTUAL SIZE 7⅜" × 6¼"

CENTER
STITCH

75

GREEK ART had a profound influence on the Romans, who often looked across the Adriatic for inspiration and artistic prototypes. The meander-like design shown here was used prominently at least twice in Pompeii—in the Temple of Apollo and as a border framing large wall paintings in the Villa of the Mysteries. In both places the original colors are white, black, and gray, although in the temple the pattern was used in a mosaic pavement and in the villa it was painted. The Romans tried to give the impression of three-dimensionality by setting off the lines in a kind of relief.

Although the scale of the design is large, it works up relatively quickly because of the use of long bargello stitches, which, in this example, should be done before the continental stitchwork. As in most designs that mix stitches, however, care must be taken to ensure that the bargello stitches lie over the continental; that is, try not to let the continental stitches pierce through the yarn of the bargello work.

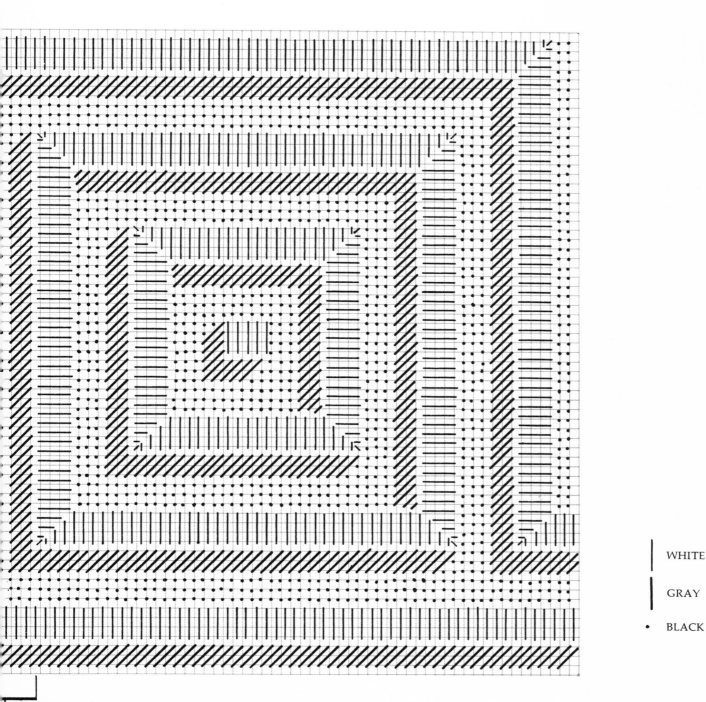

WHITE

GRAY

• BLACK

THIS PORTION OF THE GRAPH IS REPEATED.

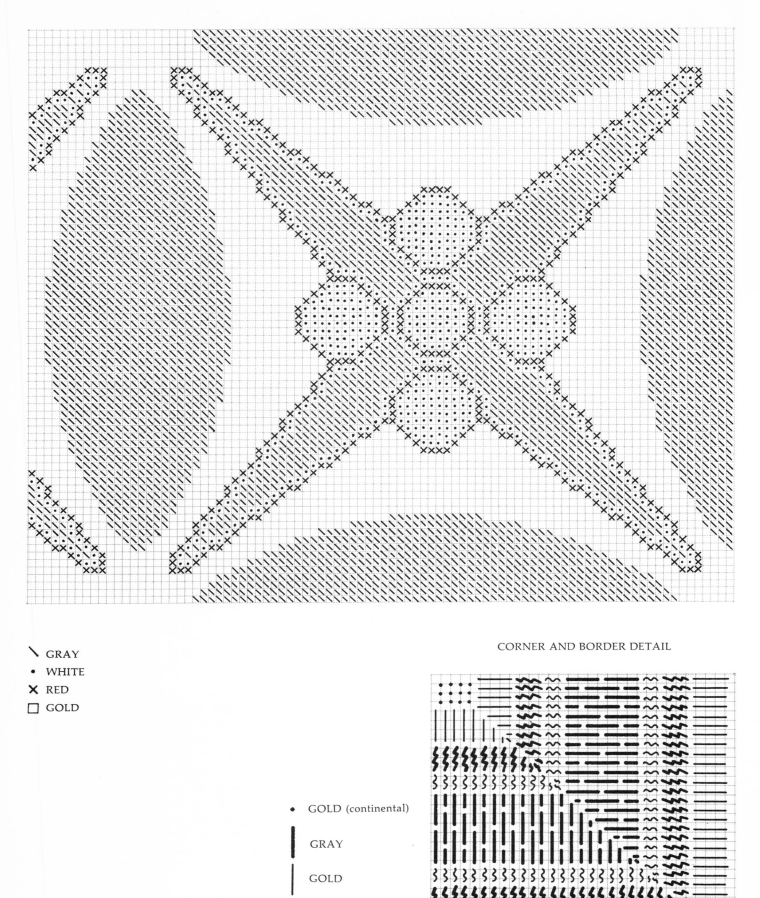

\ GRAY
• WHITE
✗ RED
☐ GOLD

CORNER AND BORDER DETAIL

• GOLD (continental)

┃ GRAY

│ GOLD

⌇ RED

∫ WHITE

ACTUAL SIZE 9⅞" × 9½"

MOSAICS composed of tesserae were not the only kind executed by Roman artists. *Opus sectile*, a kind of inlay work made of carved, specially shaped pieces of flat, colored marble, was also done. This geometrical pattern is derived from such a work that was found on the Palatine, one of the seven hills on which legendary Rome was built. The colors employed here are almost the same as those found in the original, but they have been somewhat subdued; the original also contained green, which was used to exploit the contrasts between it and the gold and red.

The border is composed of rows of bargello stitches plus a central panel executed in brick stitch, which uses four-thread-long bargello stitches with alternating starting points. Because the panel is only eight threads wide, it consists of two stitches atop each other covering four threads, each followed in the opening immediately next to it with a two-thread, four-thread, two-thread combination. The chart indicates how the stitches should be placed.

IT WAS NOT at all unusual for Roman artists to make copies of Greek artifacts. We owe much of our knowledge of Greek sculpture, for example, to Romans who copied Greek statues that have been lost. In this spirit, the design shown here is an amalgam of Roman and Greek art. The lion is an adaptation of an amphora painting by Psiax of 525 B.C. depicting Hercules strangling the Nemean lion—the first of his twelve labors. The scalloped border is Roman and was executed between the third and fourth centuries A.D. for a pavement in a villa in Genazzano. The colors used here are perhaps a bit more vivid than the ones in the original, and the area surrounding the lion's head is pinker than the original terra cotta of the vase.

Variations of this border appear frequently in Byzantine and medieval art, especially in manuscript illuminations.

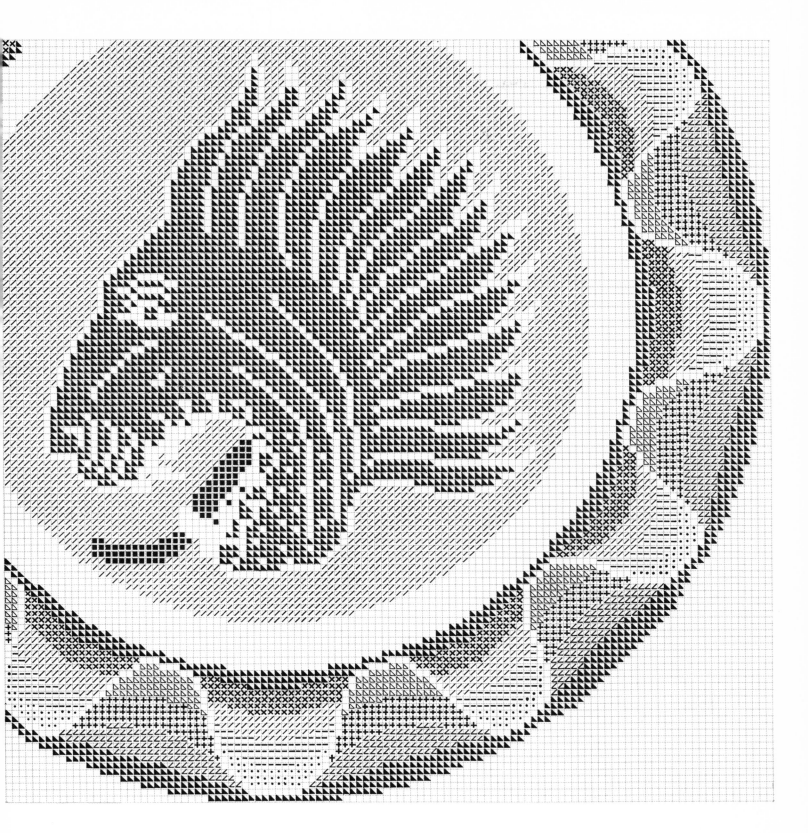

□ WHITE
∠ DARK GRAY
+ BLUE
◹ LIGHT GREY
• ROSE 4
– ROSE 3
✕ ROSE 1
∕ ROSE 2
◤ BLACK
■ PURPLE

V DESIGNS FROM THE ART OF THE BYZANTINE EMPIRE

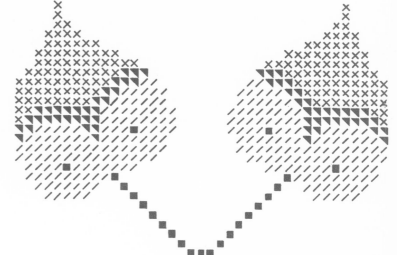

THE PERIOD OF THE BYZANTINE EMPIRE, lasting more than a millennium (A.D. 306–1453), was one of the longest in Western history. The empire was also one of the largest. At its maximum extent it encompassed territories on the southern European coast from Gibraltar to the Balkans, the northern coast of Africa, and the western part of Asia all the way to the Tigris and Euphrates rivers. Constantinople, its capital, was located strategically at the juncture of the European and Asian land masses and at the confluence of the Mediterranean, the Black Sea, and the Sea of Marmara. Its mightiest ruler, Justinian, was perhaps the most munificent patron of the arts the West has ever known. Under his aegis, countless churches were built and decorated throughout the empire, among them the Hagia Sophia, the Church of Heavenly Wisdom, an architectural masterwork that still stands in present-day Istanbul. It was Justinian who codified the old Roman laws and promulgated what has become the basis of legal systems still used in Europe (and, through the Napoleonic Code, in the state of Louisiana).

The first Byzantine emperor, Constantine, moved his capital from Rome to the old city of Byzantium on the Straits of Marmara in the year 330, after renaming the place after himself. Constantine, a Christian convert who encouraged the practice of the faith in the empire after 313, came to regard himself as God's elected representative on earth and responsible for ensuring both secular and spiritual order and purity. With the expansive embrace of the passionate convert, he called the First Ecumenical Council in 325 to establish and secure the then-diverging tenets of Christianity. Subsequent emperors believed that they, like Constantine, had been divinely appointed to perform God's will on earth. By 380 paganism was banned completely throughout the Empire, and Christianity was permanently fixed as the state religion.

Because of its location, the Byzantine Empire served as an intermediary between East and West, with extensive political and commercial power in both areas. Though the capital was heavily fortified and huge armies and navies were maintained, Byzantine emperors preferred to ensure their longevity and security through diplomatic means, with intermittent shifts of alliances, silken-voiced threats, well-placed bribes, and a network of spies. The city's location proved enormously productive to the empire, artistically as well as politically.

Byzantine art reflects a multitude of influences. Early in the life of the empire the brooding mysticism that emanated from the Near East joined with the Christian spirit that pervaded Constantine's world. The resulting fusion, enriched by the classical naturalism of the Greco-Roman tradition that was the empire's artistic heritage, produced the phenomenon known as Byzantine art.

The synthesis was a gradual one, a continuation of a trend that had been evolving for centuries. The Oriental concept of the symbolical nature of art—that a motif can exemplify an ideal—was a new notion to early Christian artists who had been inculcated with the classical idea that art need be no more than aesthetically pleasing. The development of Byzantine art, then, may in part be seen as the slow shift from the secular naturalism of Greco-Roman art toward the increasing inclusion of the more highly charged emotional and spiritual values of the Near East. The evolution may be traced in the depictions of human figures that, very early in the history of the empire, appear rather normally proportioned. Over time, however, they become characterized by too large heads, huge, staring eyes, and frontal, immobile postures. Another Near Eastern contribution to Byzantine symbolism was the use of animals like the fish, which represents Christ, the eagle, which signifies the Resurrection, and the peacock, which denotes immortality.

Cultural historians believe that the rise of Islam,

with its prohibition against artistic and religious figural representations, brought pressure on Byzantine monarchs. Many of the emperors were of Eastern origin and found the worship of saintly and divine images (but not the beatified figures and spiritual forces they depicted) an increasingly troubling phenomenon. The desire for spiritual purity, probably heightened to some degree by political considerations, resulted in a ban on religious imagery in 726. The Iconoclastic (from the Greek *ikonoklastes,* or image-breaker) period lasted for more than a century and caused the destruction of thousands of works of art and the flight of many artists to areas outside the empire, especially to Western Europe. During that time only symbols like the cross or flower and animal motifs were permitted inside churches.

Though the medium of mosaics had previously been employed by the Romans and others in the decoration of buildings, Byzantine artists brought the technique to its most exquisite use. Huge domes, ceilings, and expanses of walls were covered with tiny, colored pieces of glass and marble, perhaps a centimeter square, set into wet plaster. Possibly the greatest collection of Byzantine mosaics can be seen today in Ravenna, where the Emperor Honorius moved his Italian residence in 402. His half-sister Galla Placidia and other patrons soon afterward endowed various religious edifices in the town, all of which were richly inlaid with mosaic work. The backgrounds of the earliest mosaics were white, in the tradition of Roman art, but were later changed to blue and then, most opulent, to gold. The gold tiles, or tesserae, were made by coating slabs of glass with gold leaf and then protecting the gold surface with another thin layer of molten glass. Set into the plaster at angles slightly diverging from one another, these gold backgrounds reflect light with a shimmer that seems to dance across the surface and endow the figures on them with an otherworldly glitter.

The sumptuousness of Byzantine mosaics was extended into other arts. Carved ivories, enamels, and elaborately embroidered silk textiles were produced in Byzantine workshops. Most of these were religious works, executed for the Church, often the only patronage available for the commission of such creations.

Though the Byzantine Empire ended in 1453, its aesthetic influence continued for centuries afterward. In Greek and Balkan workshops, panel paintings of divine and saintly figures continued to be produced. A whole subcontinent was subjected to Byzantine artistic influence with the conversion of the Russian people to Christianity. Because there had been no previous Christian tradition there, missionaries both religious and artistic went out from Constantinople to Russia disseminating spiritual and aesthetic principles as they traveled. Though Byzantine influence is less easily pinpointed in the West, there had been many political contacts with the empire over the centuries and the exchange of diplomatic gifts had brought Byzantine artistic products to the West. The dispersal of artists during the Iconoclastic period and the aesthetic influence exercised upon Western artists by their travels during the Crusades also made a subtle but distinct impression on the art and architecture of Western Europe.

THE GEOMETRIC EFFECT of this pattern has been somewhat simplified from the original mosaic in the vault of the Church of Santa Costanza in Rome, executed between 324 and 326. The color of the background is slightly darker than the original, which is off-white. The pale background is an indication of the early date of the mosaic.

In such geometric designs, there is no "right" or "wrong" side—the work looks the same in any direction.

ACTUAL SIZE 7⅝" × 7¾"

✕ GREEN
◣ RED
☐ BEIGE

THIS SMALL, delicate circular motif framed many of the mosaics in the vault of Santa Costanza in Rome (including the previous design, which would appear much larger in scale when compared with this). The original off-white of the background has been brightened here and the pink, too, is a modern addition, for the original yellow is difficult to discern against such a light background.

The vault of the church is composed of eight sections, and as one progresses from the western to the eastern end, the mosaics increase in complexity from the simple geometric pattern seen previously, through two kinds of circular motifs, to large-scale designs of plants and birds. Unfortunately, the most sacred design that would have appeared in the eastern section has been lost to time.

 DARK GREEN
● RED
✕ PINK
╲ LIGHT GREEN
□ WHITE

ACTUAL SIZE 8½" × 3⅞"

ACTUAL SIZE 6⅝" × 6¾"

■ TURQUOISE
/ LIGHT BLUE
✕ GOLD
• WHITE
☐ DARK BLUE

GALLA PLACIDIA was a half-sister of the Emperor Honorius. Her mausoleum in Ravenna, from which this design is derived, is a small, outwardly unprepossessing cruciform building of red brick. The interior, however, is almost entirely paved with exquisite mosaics, most of which are set against the deep blue ground shown here. The light, filtered through alabaster panes, is subdued, and the interior radiates an ethereal quality.

This flower-like design formed a portion of the pattern in the vaulting of the mausoleum and dates from about A.D. 440. In the outer ring of the motif, eight petals alternate with eight leaflike golden crosses, while an eight-petaled flower is contained within. The number eight was a symbol of the beatitudes to the early Christians; it also signified baptism and the eighth day of creation: the Resurrection.

THE FAN-SHAPED MOTIF is a detail from an arcade arch of the presbytery in the Church of San Vitale in Ravenna, completed in the first quarter of the sixth century. This church contains the famous portrait mosaics of Emperor Justinian and Empress Theodora, each richly clad, with pearls and jewels embedded in the tesserae (though the mosaics have been extensively restored over the years).

The design does not form a full semicircle, and if doubled it would become a kind of egg-shaped motif. If you decide to use the motif just as it is charted here, I recommend that you double the bottom row of the design so that there will be two rows of yellow stitches at the base of the pattern. The original colors are altered slightly, for in the church the center half-medallion contains a gray-green shade.

ACTUAL SIZE 14⅜″ × 6½″

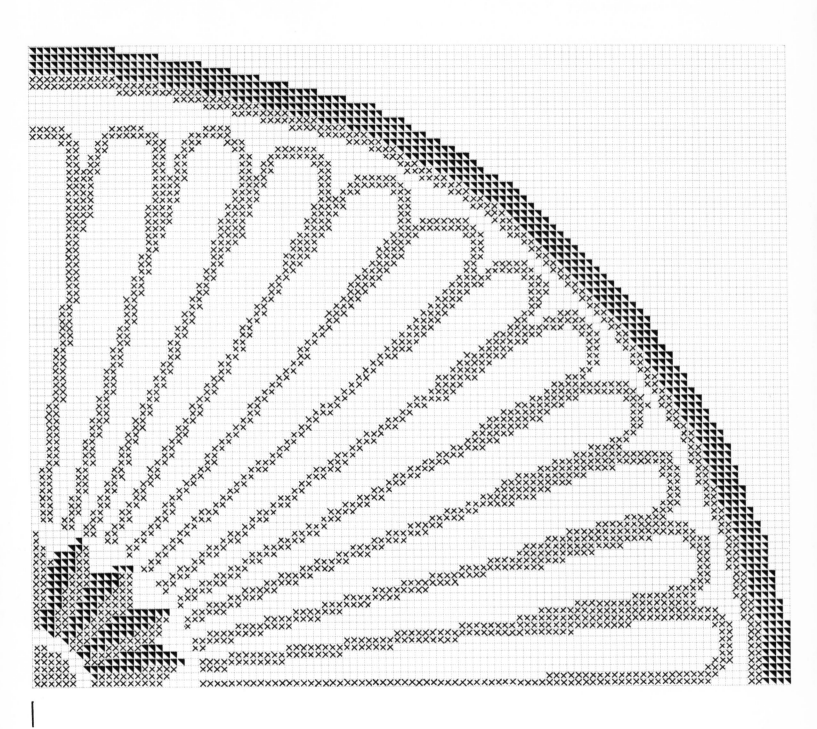

CENTER

✗   YELLOW
◢   RED
☐   BLUE

THE LETTERS *chi* and *rho,* the first two letters of the Greek word for Christ, form his monogram when superimposed. The two letters *alpha* and *omega* between the arms of the *chi* are the first and last letters of the Greek alphabet. Taken together the four letters symbolize the words of Christ in Revelation 22:13, "I am Alpha and Omega, the beginning and the end, the first and the last."

This design is derived from a silver dish made for a Bishop Paternus in A.D. 518 and now in the Hermitage Museum in Leningrad. Though the date and patron are identified by an engraving on the dish, the identity of the artist and the place of manufacture are not given. The red background is an addition; the original monogram was engraved on the silver ground.

ACTUAL SIZE 5¼" × 5½"

ACTUAL SIZE 7⅜" × 13⅞"

THE SYMBOLIC SEPARATION of the sheep from the goats on the Day of Judgment is foretold in Matthew 25: 32–34. In the metaphor the sheep are those souls who will be saved, and the goats, those who will be sent to "everlasting fire." The mosaicist of Sant' Apollinare Nuovo in Ravenna illustrated the Biblical passage in A.D. 520 in a scene showing Christ seated between the Red Angel, on his right, the sheep at his feet, and the Blue Angel, on his left, ready to lead the goats to their endless doom. Both angels are posed with right hands raised and left hands covered. Though the Red Angel was said to be enkindled with Divine Love, he presents a rather harsh visage to the modern world, while his counterpart, clothed in the blue of Divine Wisdom, appears gentle, perhaps in great sympathy with his charges, the souls of the damned.

GRAPH WILL BE FOUND OVERLEAF.

TOP

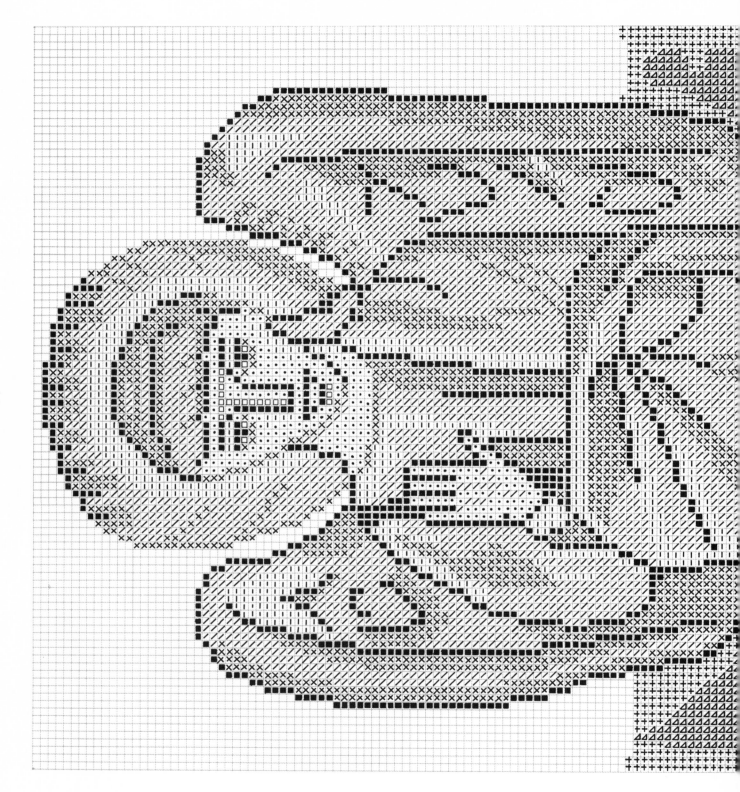

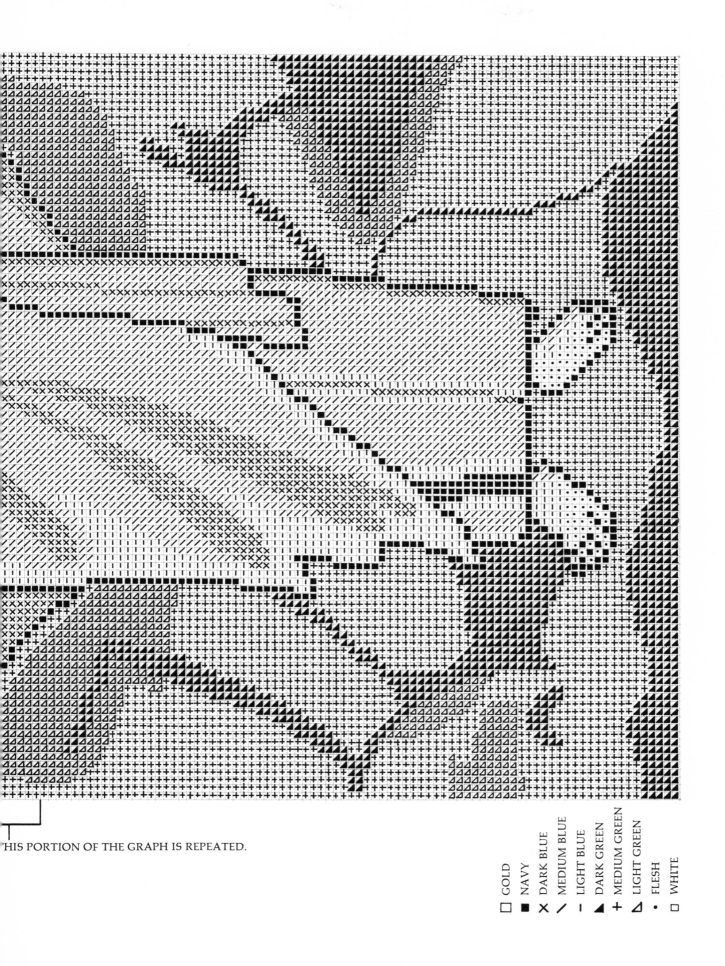

☐ GOLD
■ NAVY
✖ DARK BLUE
╱ MEDIUM BLUE
– LIGHT BLUE
◢ DARK GREEN
+ MEDIUM GREEN
◹ LIGHT GREEN
• FLESH
☐ WHITE

ACTUAL SIZE 7¾" × 8⅛"

THE USE OF the drill to achieve deeply shadowed sculptural effects and an ornamental interplay between light and dark is suggested in this motif from the capital of a column in Hagia Sophia in Istanbul, which was erected by the Emperor Justinian between A.D. 532 and 537. The Greeks and Romans usually preferred to have a solid, massive sort of capital that would appear to form a cushion between the weight above and the slender column beneath. Byzantine artists, though, enjoyed the look of lacy stonework that this leafy pattern exemplifies. The church, now a Moslem mosque, is full of such decorative effects. The capital bears witness to Justinian's patronage, for embraced by the leafy fronds that surrounded it and omitted in this adaptation was the Emperor's monogram.

CENTER

- • WHITE
- ▼ GRAY
- ☐ BLACK

95

ACTUAL SIZE 8⅝" × 4⅛"

SAINT APOLLINARIUS, a disciple of Saint Peter, was martyred in Classe, the harbor of the town of Ravenna. At the Church of Sant' Apollinare in Classe, dedicated to his memory and executed between A.D. 533 and 549, a mosaic portrays the saint at prayer.

He is seen in a landscape setting amid twelve sheep, six on either side, each separated from the next by flowering plants, with others growing beneath its feet, as in this pattern. The motif of twelve-plus-one probably symbolizes Christ and the Apostles.

■ DARK GREEN
• WHITE
⌐ RED
✕ DARK GRAY
+ LIGHT GRAY
☐ LIGHT GREEN

SCHOLARS HAVE SUGGESTED that after the destruction of the Temple in Jerusalem in A.D. 70 the interpretation of the Biblical injunction against the creation of images was relaxed slightly. Jews may then have felt freer to use religious depictions within synagogues as part of the interior decoration. In any case, the pavement mosaics from which this design was adapted were integral parts of synagogues that date from the sixth century. Because the images used here were those of ritual utensils possessed of sacred implications, not representations of human beings created in the Lord's image, perhaps no sacred laws were felt to be broken in their depiction.

The framed scene, whose Greek inscription has been translated as "Blessings to the People," was found in a synagogue in Huldah, Israel.* The largest of the five objects is the menorah, or candelabrum, described in Exodus 37: 17–24, whose branches supposedly stood for the days of creation, the seven continents, and the seven planets. It is still used today during Sabbath services. The curved object on the far right is the *shofar*, or ram's horn, whose call heralds the New Year. On the left are the *lulab*, a palm branch, in this case highly stylized, and the *ethrog*, a citron, which together symbolize the Jewish holiday of Succoth, the harvest festival. The last object is an incense shovel.

The menorah here is a substitution adapted from a pavement mosaic of the same era from the synagogue of Ma'on at Nirim, Israel, for the original was more crudely drawn. The color scheme, too, has been adapted from the Nirim pavement. The scene is framed with three rows of long bargello stitches, and the corners have been mitered for the sake of neatness.

* *Israeli Mosaics of the Byzantine Period*, Introduction by E. Kitzinger (New York, 1965).

ACTUAL SIZE 12⅞" × 9⅜"

GRAPH WILL BE FOUND OVERLEAF.

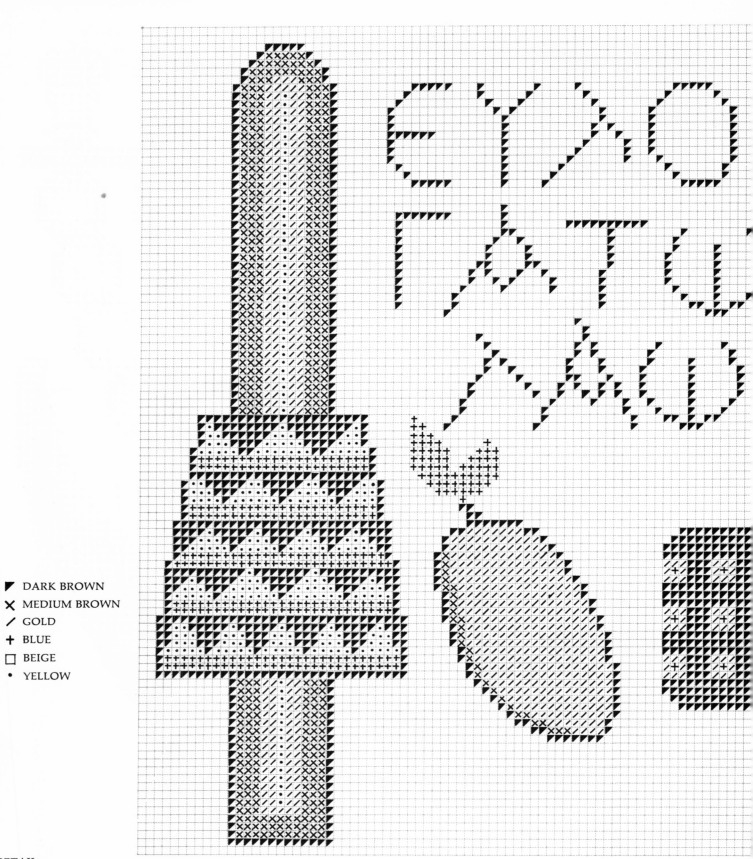

DARK BROWN

✕ MEDIUM BROWN

╱ GOLD

✚ BLUE

☐ BEIGE

• YELLOW

CORNER DETAIL

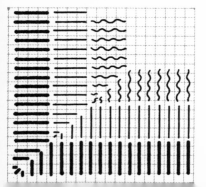

BROWN

BLUE

BEIGE

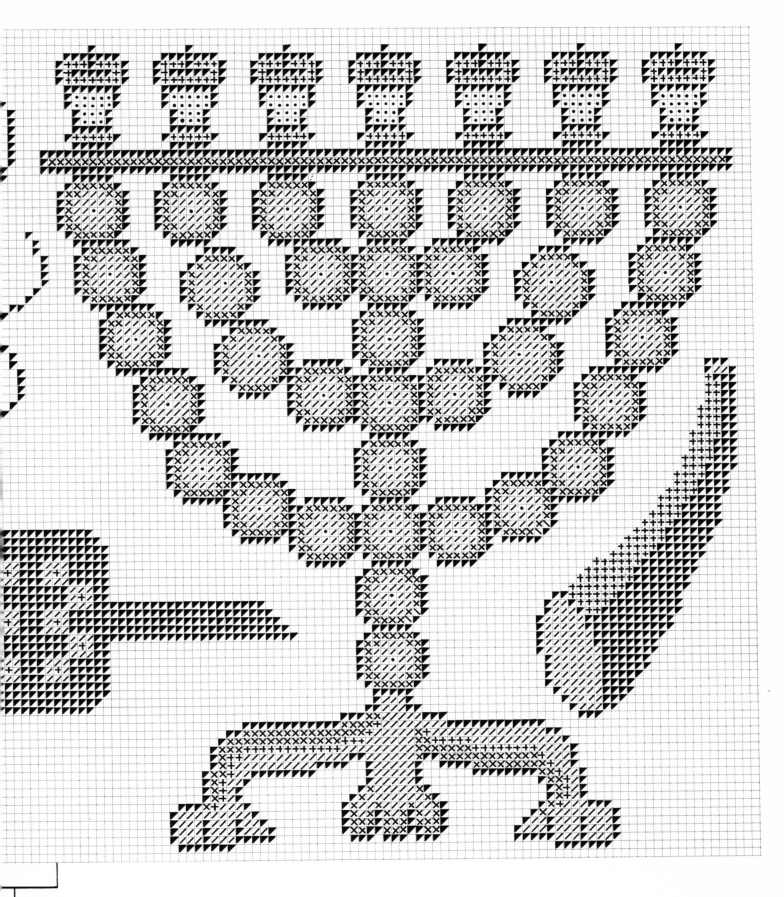

THIS PORTION OF THE GRAPH IS REPEATED.

A SIXTH-CENTURY relief sculpture of the Arch-angel Gabriel was the basis for this bargello design. The pattern of the wing feathers resembles those of a peacock, the symbol of immortality to the early Christians. Since the original material was stone, the colors in the pattern are an addition, adapted from nature.

ACTUAL SIZE 5⅛" × 6⅜"

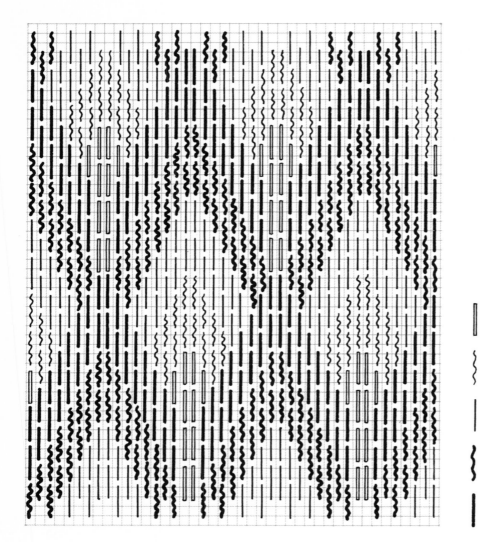

| GREEN |
| TURQUOISE |
| MEDIUM BLUE |
| PURPLE |
| DARK BLUE |

ACTUAL SIZE 3½" × 7¼"

CENTER
STITCH

◣ GREEN

✕ RED

╱ GOLD

■ BROWN

☐ WHITE

THE ORIGIN of this pattern was an Annunciation scene, framed within a circular band of flowers and woven of silk in the seventh or eighth century. The figures of the Virgin and the Angel Gabriel are set against a pale red or rose ground serving as a foil for the cream-colored band of flowers suggesting Persian antecedents. The shades used in the design of the flowers are as close to the original as modern dyes will permit, but they cannot unfortunately duplicate the hazy, delicate quality of the silk. The textile is now in the Vatican in the Museo Cristiano.

101

◢ MEDIUM BLUE
✕ GRAY
╲ LIGHT BLUE
• WHITE
☐ DARK BLUE

CENTER STITCH

THE LEAVED CROSS was a symbol used frequently during the Iconoclastic period of Byzantine art, although this particular cross, a stone relief sculpture from Salonika, Greece, dates from the tenth century, long after the period ended in 843. The symbol was also favored among the Nestorian Christians who lived in Asia east of the Byzantine domain.

Curiously enough, the leaved cross may have had religious significance at least a millennium before Christ. A tenth- or ninth-century B.C. cylinder seal now in the Louvre contains such an image and is thought to have been made by Neo-Elamites, a group living in Persia.

The cross with two arms—or double portante, in heraldic terms—is the patriarchal cross, a symbol of authority. The three steps on which the cross is placed indicate that it is the Cross of Calvary; they represent faith, hope, and charity. The pointed ends of the cross remind worshipers of the Passion, for they symbolize thorns, spears, and nails, the instruments of Christ's suffering. The arched form that frames the cross bears a resemblance to a similar motif depicted in a stucco niche from the Palace of Bishapur, a third-century Sassanian monument in Iran.

ACTUAL SIZE 7" × 9½"

103

VI DESIGNS FROM THE ART OF THE MIDDLE AGES

THE SOARING CATHEDRALS built for the greater glorification of God were the monumental works of medieval art. What was remarkable about them was not their religious inspiration—for almost all of the significant art produced until then was dedicated to the worship of divinities—but their scale and richness, which reflected basic changes in the social and economic aspects of medieval life.

During the long, dark night of centuries when Western Europe was being overrun by fierce Germanic tribes (the so-called barbarian hordes), the cherished remnants of Latin thought and culture survived, if badly frayed, in the monasteries, the sole outposts of classical civilization in the northern and western parts of the continent. The culture that emerged after the "barbarians" had been assimilated into, or themselves absorbed, the native peoples was thus like a fresh flowering of classical and Christian values.

Slowly and painstakingly the monks had copied the sacred books, the bibles and the psalters. In the process they illustrated the manuscripts, sometimes illuminating a single initial or incorporating a whole phrase within one design. The art of the manuscript illuminator, however, bore little resemblance to what had been seen in Roman art centuries earlier. A new, vital pictorial vocabulary was used by the monks of Ireland and England. The finely wrought metal work —swords and other weapons among them—that the Germanic artists ornamented with complex interlaces and zoomorphic forms were incorporated by the monks into their illuminations. The human body, which had played a central role in Greco-Roman art, was dismembered now and its shapes became elements of the new designs, alternately hidden and revealed by the overlay of pattern. Fierce, serpent-like forms twisted about each other, clutching coils in their jaws. In some illuminations, it is difficult to discern a subject from its background because of the constant imposition of motif upon motif.

With the impetus given to cultural works by Charlemagne in the ninth century, artists began to look back to Rome for inspiration. The human form, no longer fragmented, again became a focal point,

especially to manuscript illustrators, and was revitalized. Carolingian figures seem charged with the nervous energy that animated the barbarian depictions. What large-scale painting might have looked like, we do not know, for the murals and mosaics created by the artists of that time have all but disappeared.

The eleventh century, after the assimilation and conversion of the Vikings, was a time of relative tranquillity in the West. The class system of mutual obligations between master and servant called feudalism—the chain of responsibilities that linked the menial serf to the king himself—was well entrenched. The church as well was a participant in the feudal system, for it too owned lands and depended on serfs for its own support. Agriculture benefited from technological advances such as the development of a better plow, a more efficient horse collar, more economical methods of land usage, and the harnessing of natural power by the invention of the windmill. Fewer people were needed to work the land, and so a daring few among the excess population began to steal away from the farm with its constant feudal obligations to lose themselves in the towns, where, it was thought, men might be freer. Since the agricultural innovations had begun to produce a food surplus, town dwellers were able to devote themselves to the manufacture of products. Lively local trade began, augmenting the long-distance commerce in luxury goods for the nobility that had existed for centuries.

The increase in commerce, the wealth it generated, the relative political stability, and religious homogeneity combined, after the turn of the millennium, to promote a great surge of church-building activity in Western Europe. The religious impulses that ignited the Crusades also inspired other pilgrimages, many of them directed toward Santiago de Compostela in northern Spain, the supposed burial place of St. James the Apostle. Along the pilgrimage routes new churches sprang up, many of them built in the style that has come to be called Romanesque, reflecting a mélange of influences, to be sure, but perhaps more Roman than it was anything else. Often the churches were very large in order to accommodate the throngs of pilgrims who came to visit the religious relics they housed.

The Romanesque churches were ornamented with an art that had not been used since classical times, perhaps because the clergy may have seen elements of idolatry in it. The architects of Romanesque churches nevertheless began to incorporate religious sculpture in their edifices. It was unlike any ever seen by Greeks or Romans, for it was fiercely expressive, influenced in great measure by the monstrous animals of barbarian art, the geometric patterning of Islamic decoration, and mysterious oriental symbolism, all transfused and transmuted by the theme of Christianity and virtue triumphant. It must be remembered that the great masses of Western Europe were illiterate, and church sculpture acted as an illustrated Bible to educate worshipers in their religious heritage and obligations. The depictions of the Weighing of the Souls (a motif from the Egyptian *Book of the Dead*) and the Last Judgments seen in many Romanesque churches suggested the consequences for those who did not fulfill their responsibilities. The damned are shown being carried off by a pair of huge claws or dropped into Hell's gateway, occasionally represented as the mouth of an outsized beast. Much of the sculpture was also painted, an element that would have added to its realism.

Tapestries, enameling, and metal work also played roles in the decorative scheme of Romanesque churches. Because few secular examples of these arts now exist, it is believed that patrons were predominantly interested in commissioning religious works. The Bayeux Tapestry is one of the few surviving samples of what scholars think are many such large-scale embroidered or woven textiles. The goldsmith's work was often heavily influenced by church architects, for in creating suitable housing for a sacred object, the smith often fashioned a tiny golden chapel, elaborately ornamented, to serve as a reliquary.

In the middle of the twelfth century a number of architectural elements that had been used in Romanesque churches as far apart as Toledo, Spain, and Durham, England, were combined in the old province that surrounded Paris—the Île-de-France—to produce the prototype of the Gothic cathedral. The discovery that a stone building could be supported by a skeleton of stone ribs meant, to medieval architects, that for the first time the soaring spirit released by the Christian faith could be given tangible form. Cathedrals were pushed heavenward, and their walls lightened and opened up with huge stained-glass windows permitted by the new architectural principles. The movement spread outward from France (where it reached its peak in about the middle of the thirteenth century) to England, Italy, and Germany.

The sculpture that adorned Gothic cathedrals conveyed a completely different emotional message to worshipers. A spirit of relative serenity pervades Gothic sculpture. Figures seem more peaceful, no longer twisted and contorted in fear of a hellish hereafter. Parishioners were more gently induced to worship by benevolent images of Christ, the saints, and the Virgin, a maternal figure who tenderly pressed the Infant to her body. In the cathedral windows human figures were used to depict not only angels and prophets, but kings, workers, and peasants, mortals from the temporal world, where men lived and worked, glorifying through their efforts the spirit of the Almighty.

IN THE IRISH ART of the seventh and eighth centuries the convoluted interlace was a central element in many of the illuminated manuscripts produced by Celtic monasteries. One rather simple interlace is reproduced here, derived from the frame surrounding the lion, a symbol of St. Mark the Evangelist to the early Christians. In this illustration from the *Book of Durrow*, a seventh-century Irish manuscript, the colors have been changed somewhat; in the original, each element was a different shade from the one that preceded it. In this adaptation, a consistency of color and line was chosen so that a single line can be traced through a whole series of elements with ease.

ACTUAL SIZE 5⅜" × 3"

☐ RED
• YELLOW
✗ BLUE

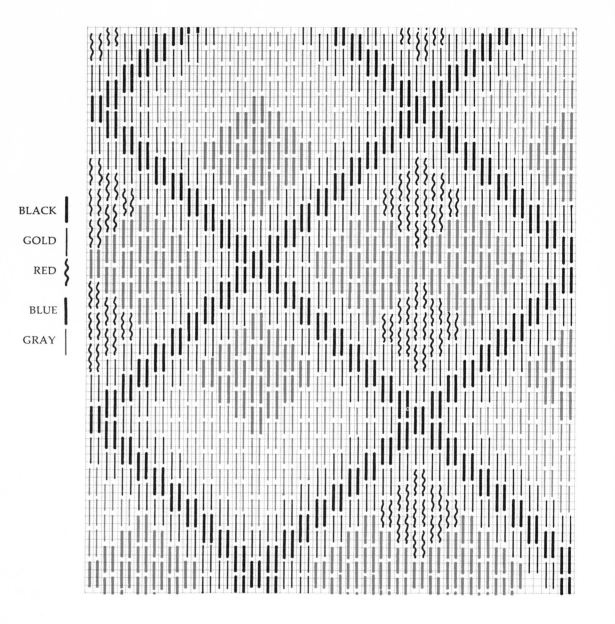

BLACK

GOLD

RED

BLUE

GRAY

THE MOST FAMOUS of all Irish manuscripts is the *Book of Kells,* named for the monastery in County Meath where the manuscript was executed late in the eighth century. This argyle pattern is derived from a detail in the manuscript portrait of St. Matthew.

The hues here are similar to the original but are considerably brighter. The pattern works up very rapidly when only long bargello stitches are used.

ACTUAL SIZE 6" × 8¼"

□ PALE YELLOW
• GOLD
✖ BROWN

ACTUAL SIZE 5¼" × 8⅜"

THE PISA CAMPANILE, or Leaning Tower of Pisa, with its arcades and columns was the starting point for this design. Because of an error in its foundation, the tower began to tilt even before it was completed at the beginning of the twelfth century. The complex of Cathedral, Baptistry, and Campanile form an outstanding example of Romanesque art, a tribute to the proud Pisans with their extensive mercantile connections.

The colors used here were chosen to evoke the interplay of the bright light and shifting shadows of the Italian province of Tuscany.

ACTUAL SIZE 10½" × 6½"

SHORTLY AFTER the Battle of Hastings, on October 14, 1066, the sole military encounter in the Norman conquest of England, a tapestry depicting the events of the invasion was begun. The finished tapestry, 230 feet long by twenty inches, was intended to be hung in the nave of the Bayeux Cathedral in order to narrate the story of the battle to the illiterate populace.

Embroidered in wool on linen using stem and outline stitches and various forms of couched work, the entire tapestry is believed to be the work of a single artist. Until the eighteenth century, tradition held that the tapestry was executed by Matilda, wife of William the Conqueror, but unfortunately, there is no record of this in the Bayeux Cathedral.

The tapestry contains over six hundred human figures, an even larger number of animals, and a great many ships, buildings, and trees. Among the animals is this pair of birds from a scene showing the Normans attacking the town of Dol, near Mont-Saint-Michel in Brittany. The birds are purely decorative, shown against a hill on which Dol's principal building is perched. They are executed here in shades close to the original against the off-white of the linen background.

110

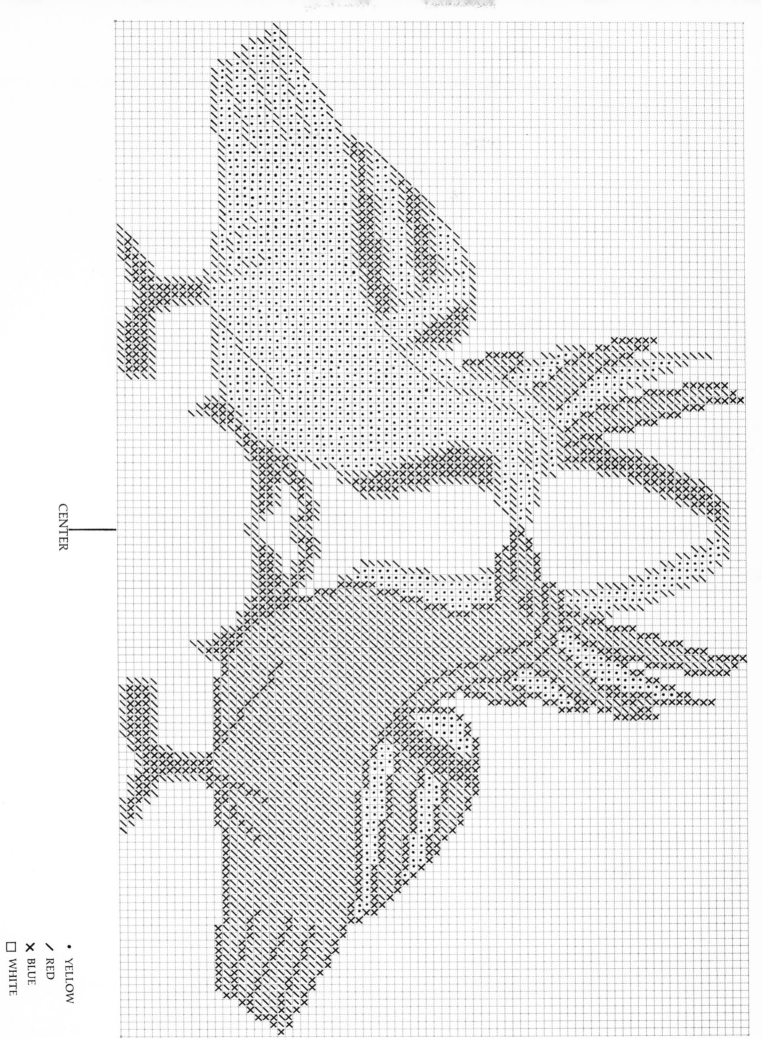

CENTER

TOP

- • YELLOW
- ╱ RED
- ✕ BLUE
- ☐ WHITE

111

BLACK

RED

GRAY

IN A CAPITAL from the church of Saint-Bertrand-de-Comminges in the Haute-Garonne in France, this interlace motif is found in stone relief sculpture. Though no date has been assigned for this capital, the area at the top of a column, it probably was executed during the eleventh or twelfth century.

The colors are, of course, an invention and the motif has been somewhat stylized in this adaptation. It works up rapidly because of the use of the brick stitch and the long bargello stitches, but one can substitute the continental for the brick stitch (though the brick stitch is used in the chart) and achieve a heightened contrast of textures.

ACTUAL SIZE 8" × 9⅝"

TOP

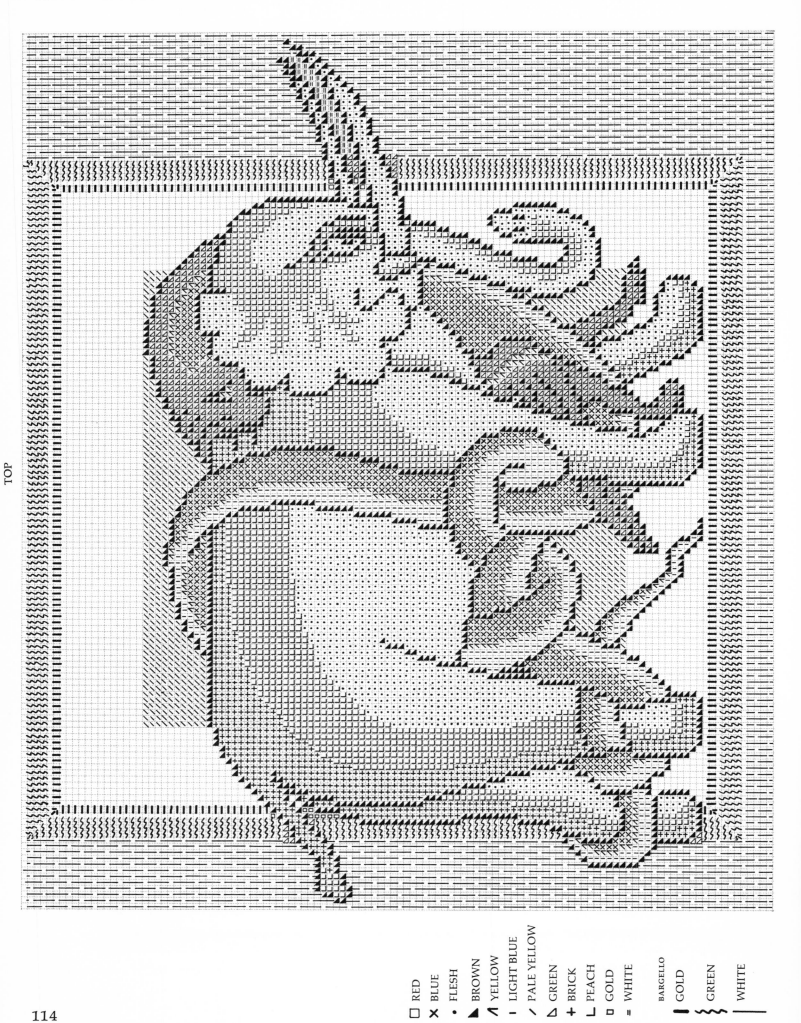

□ RED
× BLUE
· FLESH
◢ BROWN
⌄ YELLOW
I LIGHT BLUE
/ PALE YELLOW
△ GREEN
+ BRICK
L PEACH
▢ GOLD
= WHITE

BARGELLO
| GOLD
⌇ GREEN
— WHITE

THE BESTIARY, a compendium of facts about all the animals then believed to inhabit the earth, was a serious undertaking in medieval times, though to twentieth-century eyes the bountifully illustrated works often appear ludicrously fanciful. The design shown here, derived from a twelfth-century work now in the Pierpont Morgan Library, portrays a battle between a serpent and an elephant.

According to T. H. White, the author of *The Once and Future King*, who published a translation of a Latin bestiary from the same period, elephants were said to have no joints in their legs and to sleep by leaning against trees. Hunters wishing to capture one simply had to saw partially through its favorite tree so that when the elephant leaned against it, the animal would fall down and, unable to rise because of its knee-joint deficiency, could easily be taken.

Serpents, it was thought, were attracted to elephants in childbirth, and when a male elephant guarding his laboring mate saw one approach, he would try to trample it to death. With its mighty tail, the serpent could knot up the elephant's forelegs and, with its giant prey thus immobilized, was then able to thrust its head up into the elephant's trunk and suffocate it. Unfortunately for the reptile, according to the bestiary, the falling elephant was believed to crush the life from the serpent.

Some slight changes have been made from the original colors for greater visibility and contrast between the animals and the surrounding frame. In the original illustration, as here, the tusks, tail, hind leg, and serpent's coil protrude beyond the frame, extending into the margin of the paper. In the stitchery the "paper" is represented by white brick stitches, each one four threads long. The regularity of the brick stitches is interrupted by the animals' parts; one can compensate by taking smaller brick stitches—even one thread long—along the edges of the continental stitches so that the dark brown outlines are not broken.

ACTUAL SIZE 12" x 9¼"

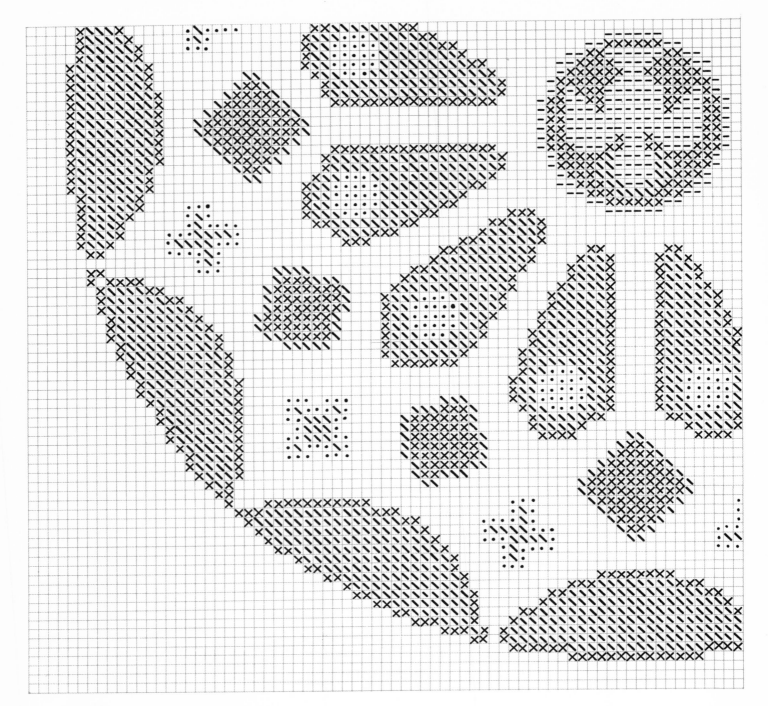

- • YELLOW
- − WHITE
- ＼ BLUE
- ✕ RED
- ☐ BLACK

THIS DESIGN is an adaptation of the rose window over the west portal of Chartres Cathedral. Built between 1194 and 1220, the cathedral is one of the finest examples of Gothic architecture.

Alive with depictions of human figures, saints, and kings in each of the window openings, the cathedral window is an awesome tribute to the glassmaker's art. In the center opening sit the Madonna and Child resplendent, surrounded by bands of shimmering red and blue light.

This adaptation is, of course, too small to include the figures. It is only in the center that religious imagery has been preserved. The Dove of the Holy Spirit, which in the original window is seen in four of the panels above the Madonna, symbolizing the four graces given to her by the Holy Spirit, here occupies the central light. The Dove is always shown head downward, since it is believed to descend from heaven. The symbol of the Dove appears in the story of Christ's baptism: "And John bare record, saying, I saw the Spirit descending from heaven like a dove, and it abode upon him" (John 1:32).

IN MANY MANUSCRIPT ILLUMINATIONS, the human figure is set against a diaper-pattern background composed of hundreds of tiny repetitive units that usually form rectangles or squares. This diaper pattern in cruciform design is adapted from a Venetian manuscript dated to the second half of the thirteenth century. In the illustration, the seated Madonna with Child on her lap are shown on a bench over which a drapery containing the motif has been thrown. The original shades were a delicate pink and white, but in this adaptation red has been substituted for greater visibility.

ACTUAL SIZE 4¼" × 4¼"

IN AN ILLUMINATION of Vincent de Beauvais's *Speculum Historiale,* Filippo de Haya, the abbot of an Italian monastary, painted the *Assembly of Nine Kings.* Arranged in a semicircle, the kings are set against an interior wall on which hangs a cloth of honor containing this diaper pattern. The illumination was probably painted during the first quarter of the fourteenth century, at the time when the abbot served as the Chancellor to Robert of Anjou, King of Naples and one of the most powerful Italian princes. The adaptation uses the original colors.

ACTUAL SIZE 6½" × 5"

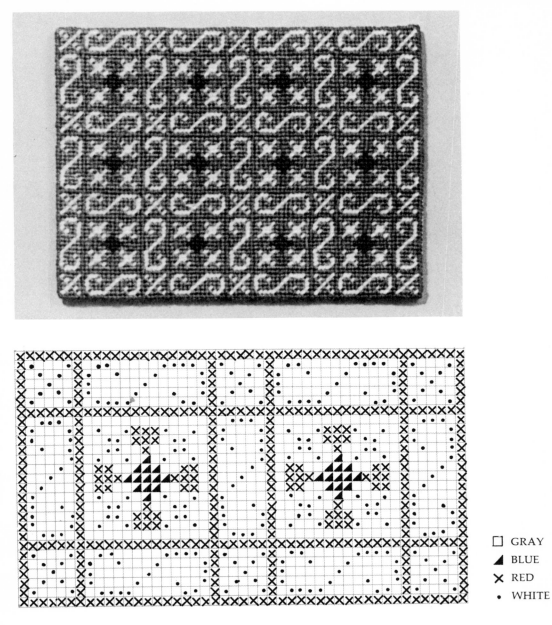

☐ GRAY
◢ BLUE
✕ RED
• WHITE

119

- • YELLOW
- ◥ BLACK
- ✕ BLUE
- ↘ GREEN
- + BROWN
- ╱ RED
- ☐ WHITE

| RED

ACTUAL SIZE 16¼″ ✕ 3¾″

120

THIS PORTION OF THE GRAPH IS REPEATED.

CENTER

ALSO ADAPTED from a stained-glass work, this design is executed in the bright, light-drenched hues of the original border of a thirteenth-century window from the Cathedral at Poitiers.

For texture and contrast, the edges of the design were worked in bargello stitch, but they can also be done equally well in continental stitch.

VII DESIGNS FROM THE ART OF ISLAM

THE ART OF ISLAM, an art predominantly of surface decoration, prohibited the depiction of human and animal forms. In reaction to the ancient Near Eastern tradition of idolatry—of imbuing such images with supernatural powers—orthodox Moslems today do not permit human and animal representations in sacred buildings.

Climate, too, has profoundly influenced Islamic art. Mohammed the Prophet, who spread the doctrine of Islam (which means submission to God), was born in Mecca, Arabia. The earliest converts to his message were natives of the arid Near East, desert regions where water is scarce and flowers are rare. The visionary notion of a garden nourished by flowing rivers became an almost sacred belief to the early Moslems. To them, Paradise (derived from the Persian *faradis* or *paradaiza*) meant a walled-in place, the finest part of a garden. Paradise was all that was beautiful, and their concept of beauty included an explosion of color, the vast fields of flowers that can be seen in Near Eastern deserts only briefly in the spring. This idealization of beauty, traditionally characterized by floral abundance, has dominated the ornamentation of sacred Islamic edifices.

Words, too, have been adapted to the decorative motifs of the mosques. Moslems believe that the Koran, the sacred book of Islam, is the Word of God transmitted to Mohammed by the Angel Gabriel. Moslem calligraphers saw the decorative potential of Arabic lettering, selected sacred excerpts from the Koran, stylized them, and thus incorporated the Word of God into the panels or friezes of mosques and other religious edifices. As Islam spread from its Near Eastern birthplace, across north Africa to Spain, to the north of present-day Turkey and eastward to India, the forms used by Moslem architects over centuries of evolution fanned outward, too. The mosque (meaning place of prostration) came to be viewed as a shelter from temporal concerns as well as a shrine to which the individual comes to speak with God. Although the mosque complex has varied in form, its characteristic features include a dome over a square chamber, a large, open vault, and an open courtyard surrounded by an arcade. It functions, moreover, as a community

center, for the mosque may also contain an elementary school, a college, a library, and, occasionally, a hall of justice.

From the inception of its architecture, the basic building material in the ancient Near East was brick. Clay construction was cheap, rapid, easily available, and adaptable for many functions. Often bricks were embellished in some way—a technique that began in antiquity with the clay cone mosaics of Mesopotamia of 4000 B.C. The method was carried forward with the glazed tiles used in a Persian ziggurat, or temple tower, of the thirteenth century B.C. Glazed, molded bricks were used in Assyria and again in Babylon in the sixth century B.C. and later in the Persian cities of Persepolis and Susa. It is not surprising, then, to see a decorative method possessed of such a long, local history used in the same region centuries later; much of the ornamentation of Islamic buildings is in the form of colored faience—that is, ceramic tiles, elaborately wrought and patterned.

As the course of Islam was given direction by the ruling caliphs who succeeded Mohammed, so too was its art. When the faith spread geographically, local elements and motifs were often included in decorative design so long as they did not conflict with Islamic proscriptions. The Umayyads, the first of the dynasties that succeeded Mohammed's leadership, were influenced by Roman techniques as well as those employed by pre-Islamic Persians. The Umayyads used simple mosaics, a Roman decorative device; painted, ornamental stucco work in geometrical and plant forms, a heritage of their ancestors, the Parthians; and patterned brick effects in the ornamentation of their buildings. Subsequent ruling dynasties employed similar techniques, although the basic artistic vocabulary, much of it originally used by the pre-Islamic Sassanians, remained the same.

Throughout the history of Islamic art, vegetative fertility has been a subtle but persistent theme. Along with geometrical patterning in brick and stucco work, the ideal of the Garden of Paradise remains a dominant decorative motif. Thousands of rosettes, vinelike arabesques, tulips, and palmettes proliferate on Moslem religious buildings, inside and out. The Tree of Life, a motif thousands of years old before the advent of Islam, survived the arrival of the new faith and was embraced within its decorative scheme. Though to Western eyes the profusion of pattern may appear crowded and confusing, the Moslem finds in it a source of contemplation and wonder, the embodiment of men's effort to thank the deity for the blessings he has bestowed.

Islamic art has had broad influence in the West. As far back as the ninth century, Charlemagne and the Caliph of Baghdad, Harun ar-Rashid, exchanged gifts. Splendid carpets and textiles woven and embroidered in Moslem lands were among the luxury goods imported for Western nobility for centuries. The Umayyads, who had established hegemony in Spain, and later Moslems who held sway there introduced motifs later borrowed by Romanesque and Gothic artists and architects. Finally, in 1492, Ferdinand and Isabella captured Granada and ended Moorish political authority on the European continent. Islamic monuments survive, though, in Córdoba, Toledo, Granada, and Seville.

Moslem artistic influence moved eastward, too. For several centuries, parts of India were under Moslem control. The Mogul dynasty, in fact, ruled for over three hundred years until its leaders were deposed in 1858. Although others exist, the most beautiful testament to Moslem rule (tempered somewhat by its Indian character) is the mausoleum Shah Jahan built in 1630–48 for the wife he called the "light of the world"—the Taj Mahal.

THE NEEDLEPOINT SAMPLES in this section are arranged in a manner different from the rest of the collection. Needlepoint, of course, lends itself beautifully to rugmaking, and because Western eyes are familiar with Islamic art principally as it has been presented in carpets, a group of predominantly architectural motifs is presented here as elements, or sections, that can be worked up together as a needlepointed oriental carpet. Each of the motifs can also be used equally well by itself. Though the designs are shown clustered, the needlepointer who wants to make a carpet should separate each of the motifs with bands of plain color so that the eye is not assaulted by a jumble of pattern and can find resting places.

All of the designs were executed on 14-mesh-to-the-inch (number 14) canvas, which is probably too fine to be used for rugs. Depending on the desired size of the finished rug, a coarser canvas—ten-, seven-, or even five-mesh rug canvas—is more practical, unless one wishes to devote the rest of one's life to the project. The fewer meshes to the inch, the greater the area covered by each stitch, of course; the charts are not affected, naturally, no matter what size canvas is used.

It is best for the sake of the longevity of the carpet to keep the stitches in it small. Large stitches invite heel-catching. Although bargello stitches have been used in these samples, they have been kept to a minimum, and tent stitches can be substituted without altering the look of the overall pattern; two tent stitches, for example, one above the other, may be used in place of a bargello stitch that covers two threads, three tents in place of a three-thread bargello stitch, and so on.

The hues in the samples are quite close to the originals; variations are noted in the captions. Much of the tile work decorating Islamic mosques is in shades of blue, turquoise, and red, as in many of the designs rendered here.

Many of us have a tendency to think of a carpet as a symmetrical entity, intended to be seen from all angles. This sort of multisided perspective is not necessarily shared by others. Because many oriental carpets were woven originally as prayer rugs, they were woven "right side up" from just a single side. These are rugs that contain the "prayer niche," or *mihrab*, an arch-shaped form that is always placed facing toward Mecca. One must also remember that these rugs were made not only by artisans in the royal workrooms of imperial palaces but also by nomadic tribesmen who were furnishing their own homes. As a result, one can occasionally find a kind of insouciant awkwardness in the arrangement of the patterns of an oriental carpet that manifests itself particularly in the treatment of corners. Because the central field takes precedence over the border in a rug, one can often find, in following the border pattern along the edge, that a motif ends abruptly when a corner is turned, whether or not the motif was woven in its entirety.

In the spirit of this tradition, no attempt was made to make the border patterns shown here "turn the corners." Anyone choosing to fashion a rug based on these designs is likely to have a quite specific size in mind, and it is thus most sensible to continue the convention established centuries ago in the Near East: when the edge of the canvas is reached, just break off the pattern, turn the canvas ninety degrees, and begin the pattern again.

ACTUAL SIZE 11¾″ × 11¾″

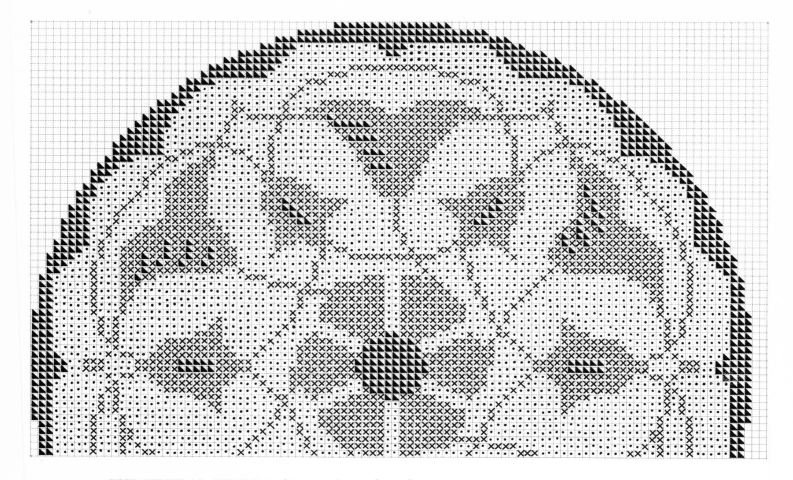

1. THE CENTRAL CIRCLE in this sample is adapted from a detail in the tile work in the mausoleum of Süleyman the Magnificent in Istanbul, executed in the sixteenth century. The background of the original is a lapis lazuli blue, and the tulips and rosette are white against the blue ground. Here the colors have been reversed.

- • OFF-WHITE
- ✕ NAVY
- ◣ RED
- ☐ MEDIUM BLUE

DETAIL: SEE COMPLETE
PHOTOGRAPH ON PAGE 125.

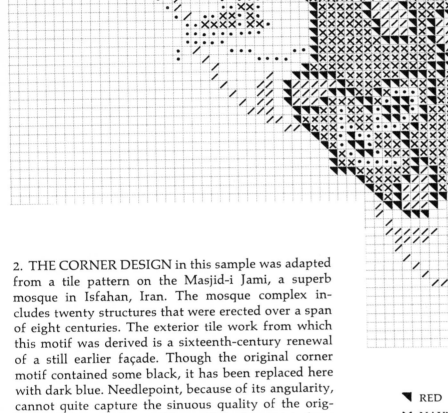

2. THE CORNER DESIGN in this sample was adapted from a tile pattern on the Masjid-i Jami, a superb mosque in Isfahan, Iran. The mosque complex includes twenty structures that were erected over a span of eight centuries. The exterior tile work from which this motif was derived is a sixteenth-century renewal of a still earlier façade. Though the original corner motif contained some black, it has been replaced here with dark blue. Needlepoint, because of its angularity, cannot quite capture the sinuous quality of the original arabesques, the vinelike tendrils that twist about each other and surround the corner medallion.

Since the purpose in this section is to provide the nucleus for a neo-oriental carpet, the corner pattern was scaled to surround the central circle to form a square, but it might be used to form a decorative corner of a square or rectangular design of any size. For example, if a large-scale rug is contemplated, one might use the center circle four times (two circles by two circles) to form a square pattern, or six times (two circles by three circles) to form a rectangular central field. No matter how many circles are made, the corner pattern can be used to anchor them and help make the transition from central field to the rectangularity of the borders. One must be extremely careful, however, to count the number of stitches along the sides of the motif and from the corner to the center of the design in order to avoid superimposing the corner pattern over a central one. In any case, it is always best to allow for errors and give oneself a little extra canvas just to be safe when planning a design of this sort.

▼ RED
✕ NAVY
╱ LIGHT BLUE
• OFF-WHITE
□ MEDIUM BLUE

DETAIL: SEE COMPLETE PHOTOGRAPH ON PAGE 125.

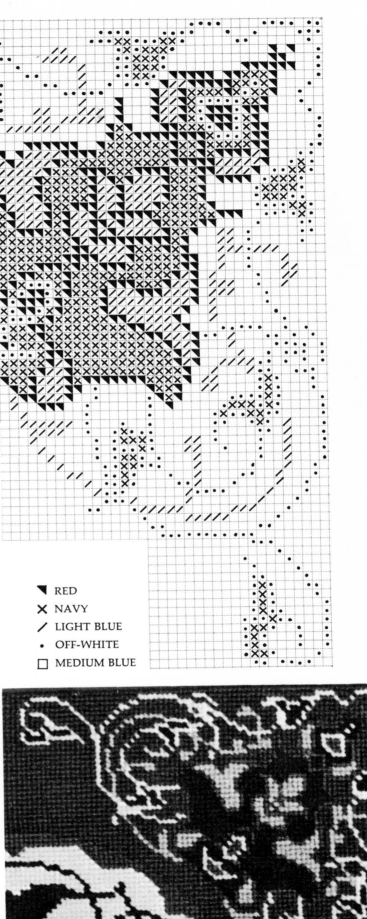

ACTUAL SIZE 15½" × 21"

3. THE PATTERN AT THE TOP of this sample is derived from the colored tile work on the dome of the Bab Zuwella, a mosque in Cairo dated to about the fourteenth century. The color scheme is somewhat brighter than the original tiles. Here is an instance where one can substitute the tent stitch for the longer bargello stitch, if desired, using two tent stitches in place of a single bargello stitch throughout the design.

DETAIL: SEE COMPLETE PHOTOGRAPH ON PAGE 128.

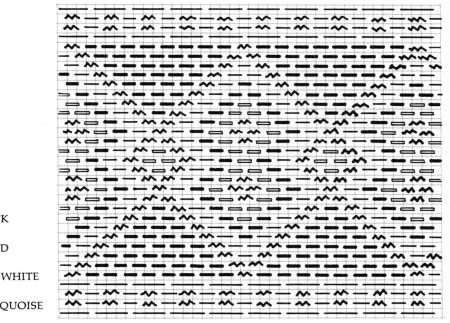

{ BRICK

| GOLD

| OFF-WHITE

| TURQUOISE

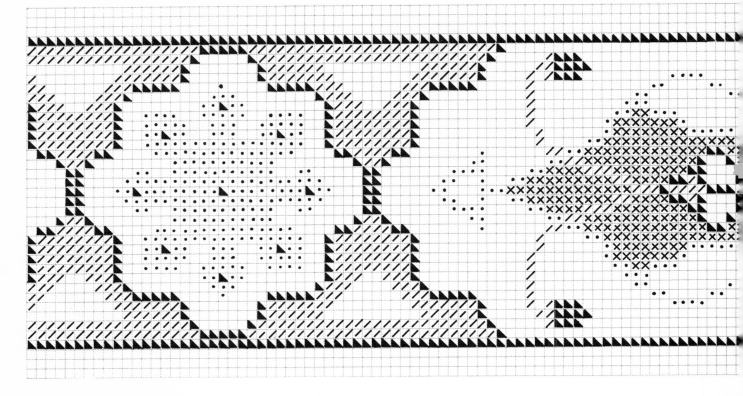

4. ANOTHER DETAIL from the Masjid-i Jami in Isfahan forms the basis for this design. Except for the turquoise, a substitution for the original gray-green, the other shades are similar to the original ones.

DETAIL: SEE COMPLETE PHOTOGRAPH ON PAGE 128.

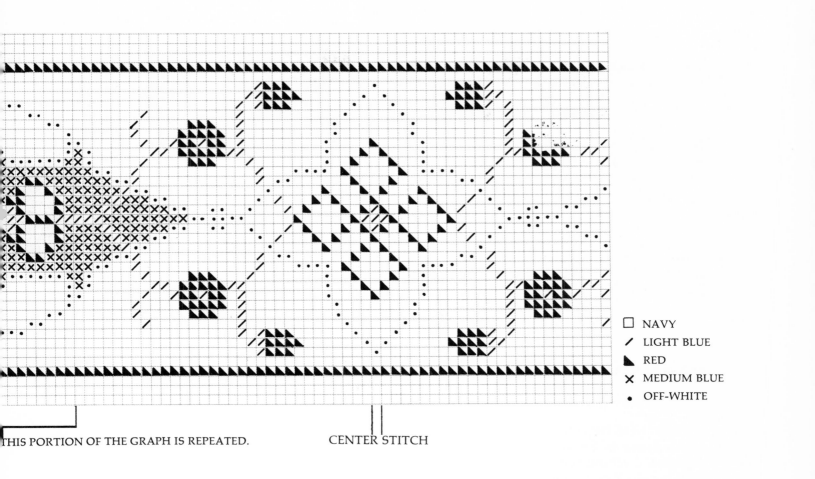

NAVY

/ LIGHT BLUE

◣ RED

✗ MEDIUM BLUE

• OFF-WHITE

THIS PORTION OF THE GRAPH IS REPEATED.   CENTER STITCH

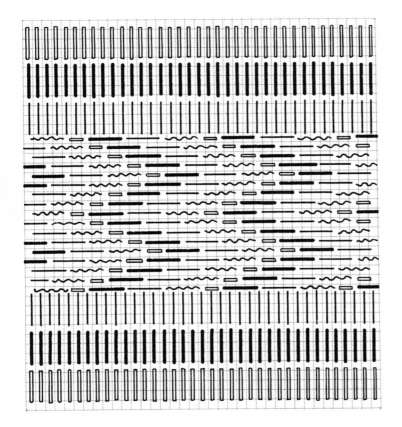

⌇ GOLD

▯ OFF-WHITE

▮ NAVY

▮ RED

DETAIL: SEE COMPLETE PHOTOGRAPH
ON PAGE 128.

5. A TENTH-CENTURY woven silk textile border
pattern has been reproduced in this motif. Blue has
been used instead of the original black, but because
of the extreme age and delicacy of the piece it is hard
to determine what the exact shades of the original
hues may have been. The silk is now in the Louvre
collection.

6. CARPETS have been made in the Near East for millennia. The oldest examples found date back to the fourth century B.C., and Assyrian relief sculptures suggest that they may even antedate that. These stylized birds, for so they have been called, were derived from a fragment of a more recent carpet, a thirteenth-century woolen one found in a mosque in Konya, Turkey, currently in the Ethnographical Museum there. In the fragment the birds are placed in rows both vertically and horizontally and seem to be randomly colored red, with a white outline separating them from the red background, white and blue. The ground of the original has a somewhat yellower cast than this adaptation. All of the birds are seen in profile and face in the same direction (left), while the branching shapes colored white and blue in the adaptation seem to represent wings.

DETAIL: SEE COMPLETE PHOTOGRAPH ON PAGE 128.

✗ NAVY
• OFF-WHITE
□ ROSE

7. IN THE WAKE of Moslem military victories, mosques were built in conquered lands. The source of this motif is a detail from the seventeenth-century mosque of Wazir Khan in Lahore, India. Again, to conform to other shades used in the sample, the black of the original has been changed to dark blue.

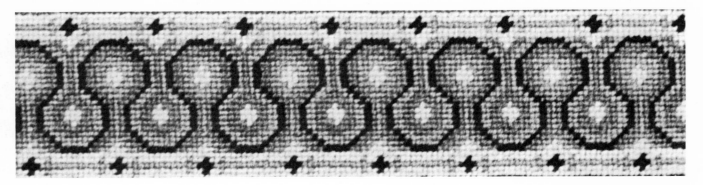

DETAIL: SEE COMPLETE PHOTOGRAPH ON PAGE 128.

▲ NAVY
• LIGHT BLUE
✕ ROSE
☐ OFF-WHITE

8. THIS SEGMENT is based upon a tile detail from the fifteenth-century Blue Mosque in Tabriz, Iran.

9. THE UMAYYADS established themselves in Spain in the eighth century and made their capital at Córdoba, a city that still bears witness to the Moslem tenancy. The intricate red and white brick-work decoration of the Great Mosque, one of the buildings still surviving from the tenth century, was the source of this bargello design.

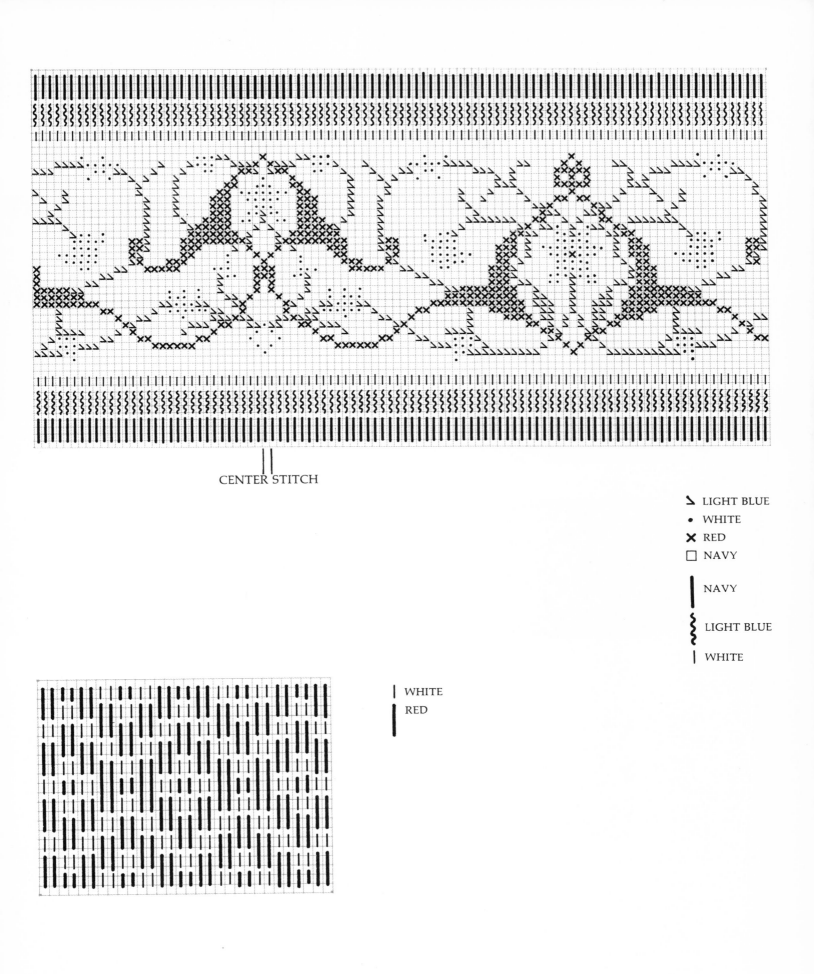

CENTER STITCH

ACTUAL SIZE 3⅛" × 15¾"

10. AN ENTRANCE to the Masjid-i Jami in Isfahan was lined in tile work in this pattern. Though the Moslems used only the four colors shown, the motif might be used with as few as two or an infinite number because of the subtle manner in which transitions between the hues are made.

	TURQUOISE
	OFF-WHITE
	NAVY
	RED

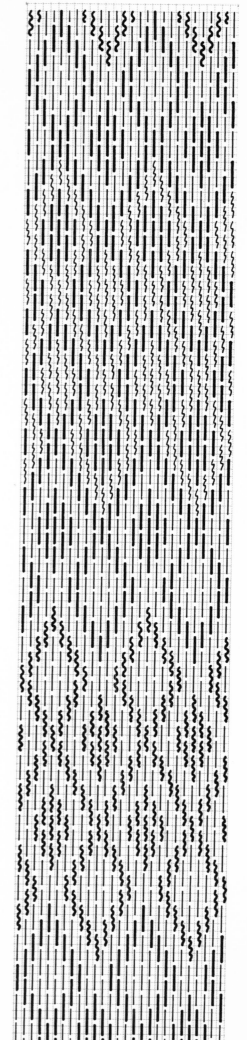

VIII DESIGNS FROM THE ART OF THE RENAISSANCE

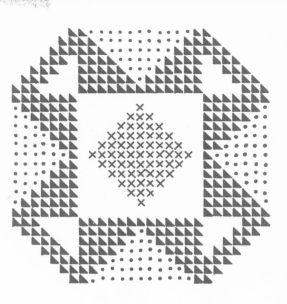

THE THOUGHT that anyone may contain within him the seed of greatness nourished the remarkable blossoming of the arts and sciences that has come to be known as the Renaissance. The authority of the Church receded as the Western European of six or seven centuries ago gradually began to regard his life on earth as more important than the afterlife that awaited him. What mattered was the reality that one could see around him: the expansion of towns and trade, the increase of wealth, and the growing prestige and power of men who, by their own individual effort, not by accident of birth, achieved acclaim. Accomplishments that ranged from the battlefield victories of the *condottiere* Federigo da Montefeltre, Duke of Urbino, to the poetry of Dante Alighieri were celebrated as paradigms of human endeavor. The belief in man's unbridled potential was manifested in the art of the vanguard areas of Italy and Flanders. The newly noted architectural remnants of the Roman Empire reminded Italians of an ancient greatness and impelled them to match or surpass their forebears. In the Lowlands of Northern Europe, bereft of classical remains, the self-confidence generated by people who could see their own material accomplishments proliferating was stimulus enough to enable them to sustain their efforts. In both areas the humanist impulse was reflected in the extraordinary number of portraits that were painted—artistic statements memorializing the lives of the newly rich and powerful.

Women were not excluded from equal consideration during this turbulent era when their role, among the upper economic strata, was as great as that of men. Italians of both sexes were often given the same education, and, while unmarried women were usually kept secluded, married ones could and did conduct themselves with the same freedom as their men friends. Just as one's mental capacities were supposed to be explored and developed to their fullest, so it was with one's physical attributes. In Italy, both sexes used perfumes, plasters, paints, and false teeth made of ivory. So much money was lavished on wardrobes that in Venice laws were passed to regulate dress. Blond hair was considered particularly beautiful, and dyes and sunbathing were indulged in to achieve it.

When these methods failed, false hair of white and yellow silk was worn by women, and it was not unknown for men as well to wear wigs.

Though we tend to regard many Renaissance artists as geniuses and a group apart, their contemporaries did not. Artists were paid neither more nor less tribute than other members of society; they were thought of simply as people who made their living with brushes instead of hammers and saws—fellows who lived around the corner or down the street. In fact, we refer to one of the first Renaissance giants by the nickname given to him by his Florentine friends—the artist known to us as Giotto. The typical artist of the time was apprenticed at twelve or thirteen and was rated a master painter in his twenties. By contemporary standards, he was bourgeois, maintaining a shop to receive patrons, a staff of paid assistants, and obligatory membership in his craft guild. Clients were charged on the basis of the cost of materials and the amount of time spent on their commission. Though many artists were in the employ of royal courts, most were free agents, able to accept any commissions they might be offered—from the glamorous diplomatic missions given to Jan van Eyck by Philip, Duke of Burgundy, to paint portraits of women he was considering marrying, to less aggrandizing work such as painting and gilding sculpture carved by another artist (a commission also accepted by van Eyck). During the Renaissance, then, the artist was scarcely an exalted minor deity but simply a virtuoso in his chosen field.

Delight in the natural world and in one's immediate surroundings was a development complementary to the emphasis on the individual in Renaissance art. The Crusades had opened the eyes of Western Europeans to the wonder of exotic places, and that sense of fascination with the temporal world was gradually extended to include domestic as well as alien settings. The realism that suffuses the painting of Flemish masters and the inclusion of the tiniest details were to influence the Italian artists of the fifteenth century who believed that van Eyck had been able to capture the very soul of the natural world. This pervasive insistence on realism was extended to religious art as well as secular. During the Renaissance a figure new to religious iconography appeared—Joseph, taking his place alongside the Virgin and Child in depictions of the Holy Family and thus mirroring contemporary society's own familial arrangements. The Mother now visibly adores her Child with gentle and tender caresses, nursing the babe before the warmth of the fire in a domestic interior that resembles a middle-class home. Occasionally in the art of the past, the donors of a religious work were included in the painting as tiny, subsidiary images far distant from the sacred figures. During the Renaissance, by contrast, the holy figures, dressed in contemporary fashion, were removed from a heavenly context, painted in the same scale, and placed in the same setting as that of the donors—the world the artist saw around him. Nudity was no longer reserved solely for images of negative value—Adam and Eve, for example, and the souls of the damned. Because the nude human body was now recognized as a fact of daily life, it became permissible to show even the crucified Christ, most sacred of images, clad only in loincloth.

Artists of the Renaissance were fascinated by the discovery, made early in the period, that light (and its absence, shadow) could be used with remarkable effect to imply the shape of forms, to model them and increase their three-dimensional character. Textures as diverse as brass and wood could be painted with greater verisimilitude as the artist captured the quality of the light reflected from each. Painters conceived their works with the sense that in almost all cases, but particularly in landscape settings, a single source of illumination should pervade the renderings and that shadows should be painted in consonance with the direction of that light.

Renaissance aesthetic theorists generally conceived of the painted surface as a portion of space viewed through an opening, or a sort of window. The frame around the painting thus became an intermediary device between the reality that existed outside of the painting and the dynamic realism achieved within it. In order to emphasize the transition between reality and realism, Jan van Eyck, perhaps the greatest artist of the Northern Renaissance, painted his frames with the look of marble, setting off the created scene yet allowing the viewer to make a gradual passage toward it.

In a further advance of perspectival rendering, artists of the era realized that they could portray objects, landscape elements, or architecture as if thrust far back into the space directly opposite the viewer. Perspective was also applied to the human figure, as arms, legs, and torsos were pushed forward or backward, painted with all of the angles that human parts were capable of assuming. The artist's viewpoint, too, might change radically from one work to another, as he contemplated and recorded a scene from above or below or the side. Figures were shown to overlap each other—evidence that the depicted bodies were real enough and occupied palpable space. And despite the jewel-like landscapes of the Flemish masters, with their almost microscopic detail, the artists of the Renaissance finally realized that beyond a certain point in the visible distance, the colors of sky, field, and mountain tend to "gray out" and shapes fade; one cannot, finally, see forever.

Part of the reason that the Flemish were able to achieve such remarkable detail was their discovery of oil paints long before the Italians. It was customary in Italy to use a water-soluble tempera paint, the finely ground pigment blended, or tempered, into a paste made of egg yolk. This produced a relatively opaque medium, fast-drying so that brushstrokes could not be blended into each other. In Flanders, oil paint was found to be slower to dry, but it allowed brushstrokes to achieve a smooth consistency and high degree of translucence on the surface. It was van Eyck who discovered that by covering an opaque paint with an oil paint, greater depth and intensity could be achieved through the reflection of light from the double-layered surface.

▲ ▲

Though the convulsive economic and social changes that swept across Europe at the time of the Renaissance were mirrored in the art produced in Italy and Flanders, there were, of course, important differences between the two areas. Italy, surrounded by reminders of the Greeks and Romans and hungry for a return to the greatness those ruins evoked, tended to portray the ideal forms of classical art. They painted human beings the way they were supposed to look. The Flemish, perhaps because there was little classicism in their artistic heritage, painted people as they were, with all their imperfections. Perhaps that is why we may admire and aspire to the greatness of the Italian Renaissance artists, but in the individualized art of the Northern Renaissance, we may see a likeness of ourselves.

THIS CHECKERBOARD DESIGN interspersed with geometric motifs is an adaptation of the floor-tile pattern of Jan van Eyck's *Madonna of Chancellor Rolin*, painted about 1434. Although the drapery around the central figures hides all but a small portion of the floor, the artist was careful to leave several visual clues that allow the viewer to infer the entire pattern. The small chart included here indicates the overall effect of the floor. The portion of the floor that has been stitched in the sample is the sixteen squares of the upper right corner.

The design has been stitched in shades that are close to but brighter than the original ones. The solid-color squares have been executed in a variation of the scotch stitch in order to present a textural contrast to the squares with the geometric motif. The stitch is simply a bargello stitch done on the diagonal, as can be seen on the chart, but these squares can also be done in the tent stitch, if desired.

ACTUAL SIZE 8" × 8"

1

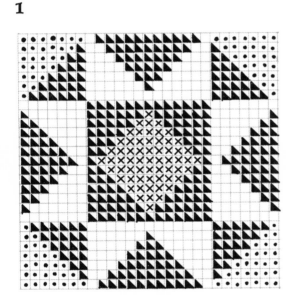

2

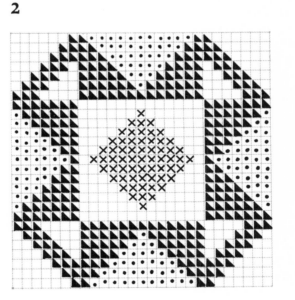

▲ BLACK
● COPPER
□ TAN
✕ BRICK

A B C

VAN EYCK'S FLOOR SCHEME

2 A 1 A 2 A 1 A 2
C B A B C B A B C
1 A 2 A 1 A 2 A 1
A B C B A B C B A
2 A 1 A 2 A 1 A 2
C B A B C B A B C
1 A 2 A 1 A 2 A 1
A B C B A B C B A
2 A 1 A 2 A 1 A 2
C B A B C B A B C
1 A 2 A 1 A 2 A 1
A B C B A B C B A

BRICK STITCH

A = Black Square

B = Tan Square

C = Brick Square

COMMISSIONED TO DECORATE the refectory wall of Santa Croce in Florence in the mid-fourteenth century, Taddeo Gaddi surrounded the central scene depicting the Tree of the Cross with a border consisting in part of repetitions of the motif shown here. Though the gray, white, and pale reds of the central portion of the design were constantly adhered to, the artist alternated the ground colors, and used both the pale green of this pattern and a pale orange.

ACTUAL SIZE 19¼" × 4⅛"

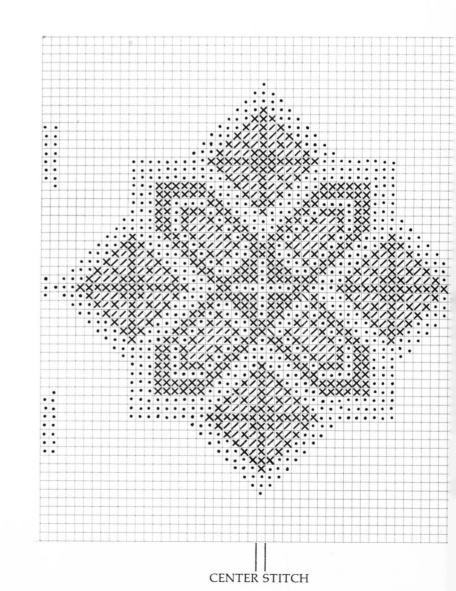

- • WHITE
- ◤ GRAY
- ✗ DUSTY ROSE
- ╱ PINK
- ☐ LIGHT GREEN

CENTER STITCH

ACTUAL SIZE 8½″ × 5½″

ARTISTS OF THE RENAISSANCE adored opulent fabrics and lavished enormous care on their depictions of velvet, damask, and brocade. The patterns contained in the fabrics were often of oriental origin—variations of palmettes, for example—even though by the fourteenth and fifteenth centuries such fabrics were produced in workshops in Genoa, Lucca, and Venice.

In his *Massacre of the Innocents*, executed in 1482, Matteo di Giovanni, a Sienese, exhibits the Renaissance artist's preoccupation with beautiful fabrics by clothing Herod in what appears to be a lavish silk robe. This design is a derivation of the robe pattern, in shades close to the artist's original conception.

The stitches are tent and bargello and one not used here previously—the double leviathan. By counting threads of the canvas and using the numbers on the chart, one can see at just what points the needle must go down through the canvas and emerge from it.

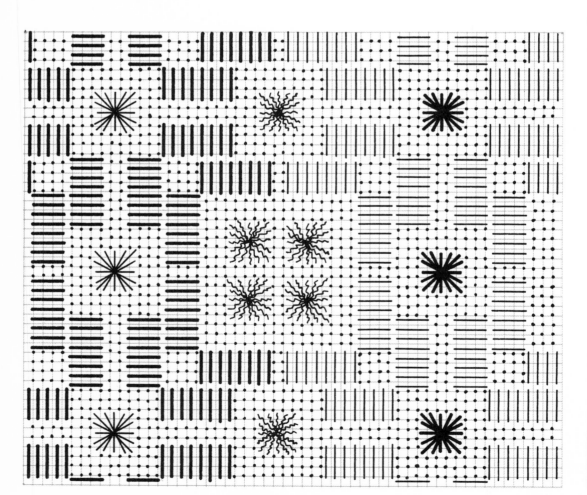

	DARK GREEN
	LIGHT GREEN
	RED
•	PEACH (continental stitch)

DOUBLE LEVIATHAN STITCH: Needle out of canvas at odd numbers, needle into canvas at even numbers.

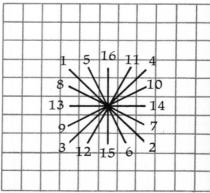

THIS HARE is adapted from the second tapestry of the series, *The Unicorn at the Fountain*. It, too, possesses a symbolism both secular and religious, for though the animal represented fertility, it also came to stand for men who, like the hare, were defenseless and had to put their hope for eternal salvation in Christ.

Because it was so small, the hare has been executed in 10-mesh-to-the-inch canvas so that details of shading could be seen more easily. The hare's eye was originally black, which looked very harsh against the gray, so a dark violet has been substituted.

ACTUAL SIZE 6⅜″ × 7⅝″

- • PALE GRAY
- ◣ DARK VIOLET
- – LIGHT GREEN
- ✗ DARK GREEN
- ∠ DARK GRAY
- ＼ MEDIUM GRAY
- ☐ NAVY

143

MANY AN ARTIST of the past survives only through his work; his name is lost to time and the vagaries of fame in ages that cared little for the achievement of lone creators. So it was with the Master of Flémalle, the name associated with a series of paintings presumed to have been executed in that Belgian town, near Liège, by a man who was, beyond dispute, among the earliest of the great Flemish painters. Among his works was an early fifteenth-century painting known as *Madonna in a Domestic Interior* from the Salting Collection in the National Gallery, London. In it, the Madonna, her head haloed by the woven straw firescreen behind her, is seen nursing her Child and, over her shoulder, an open shutter reveals a townscape that formed the basis of this design. The entire painting measures only 25 by 19.2 inches, so the scene that has been adapted here is less than five inches high.

The needlepointed landscape suggests two of the artistic concepts that characterized the Renaissance in Northern Europe: an insistence upon minute detail and, as one might deduce from the frame around the scene, a delight in perspectival rendering—that is, an attempt at showing *precisely* how figures or objects look from a particular vantage point.

The brown frame, executed in brick stitch, is a replica of the interior framing of the window, which would appear as if one were standing directly in front of it. It is the gray frame, also done in brick stitch, that makes the transition between the interior and exterior walls of the building and enables one to see how the perspective was achieved. The artist's eye was plainly fixed above the midpoint of the scene (for the lower transitional frame is seen in full while the upper one is completely hidden) and somewhat to the right of the window (one sees more of the left frame than the right). Some subtlety has necessarily been lost in adapting the scene for needlepoint. The townscape can, of course, stand on its own without a frame at all.

TOP LEFT
CORNER

BARGELLO DETAIL

TOP RIGHT
CORNER

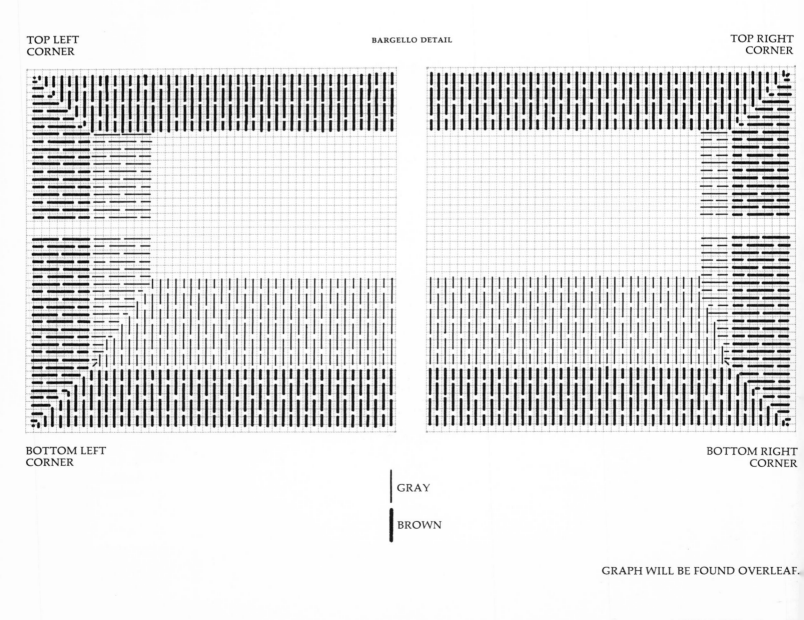

BOTTOM LEFT
CORNER

BOTTOM RIGHT
CORNER

GRAY

BROWN

GRAPH WILL BE FOUND OVERLEAF.

ACTUAL SIZE 11" x 16½"

TOP

PALE BLUE

MIDDLE BLUE

	MAROON		LIGHT GREEN
	DARK GRAY		ROSE
	BLACK		TAN
	TAUPE		MEDIUM GRAY
	BRICK		ORANGE
	PALE PURPLE		PINK
	DARK GREEN		LIGHT GRAY
	WHITE		

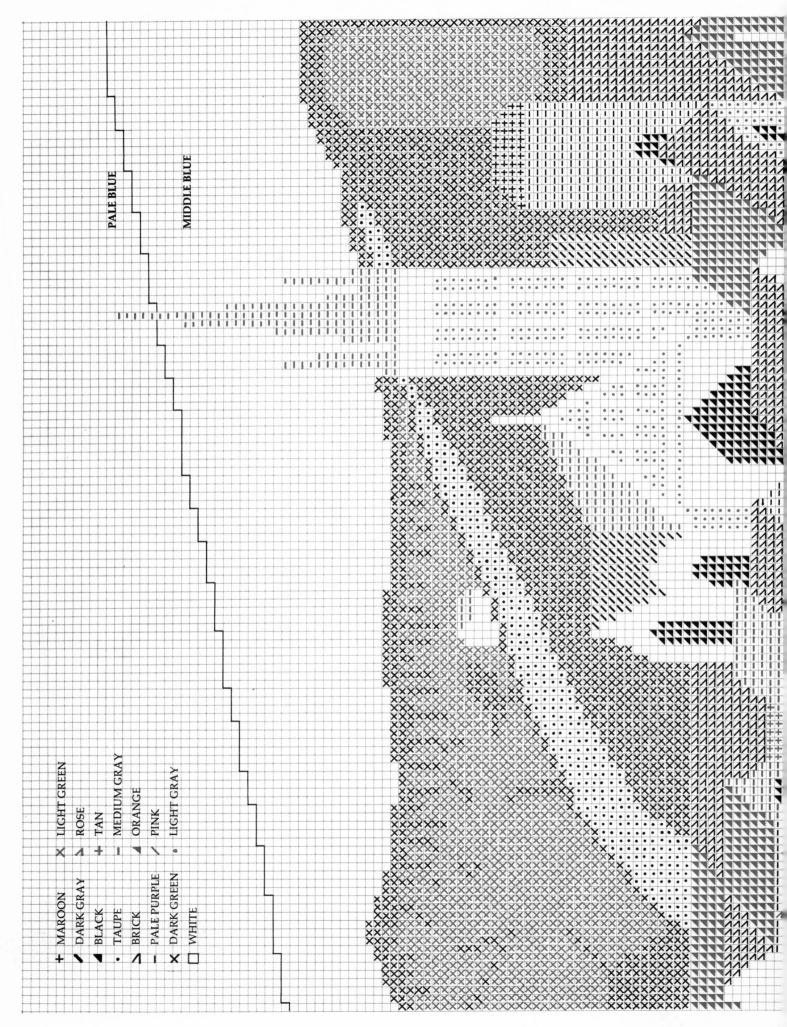

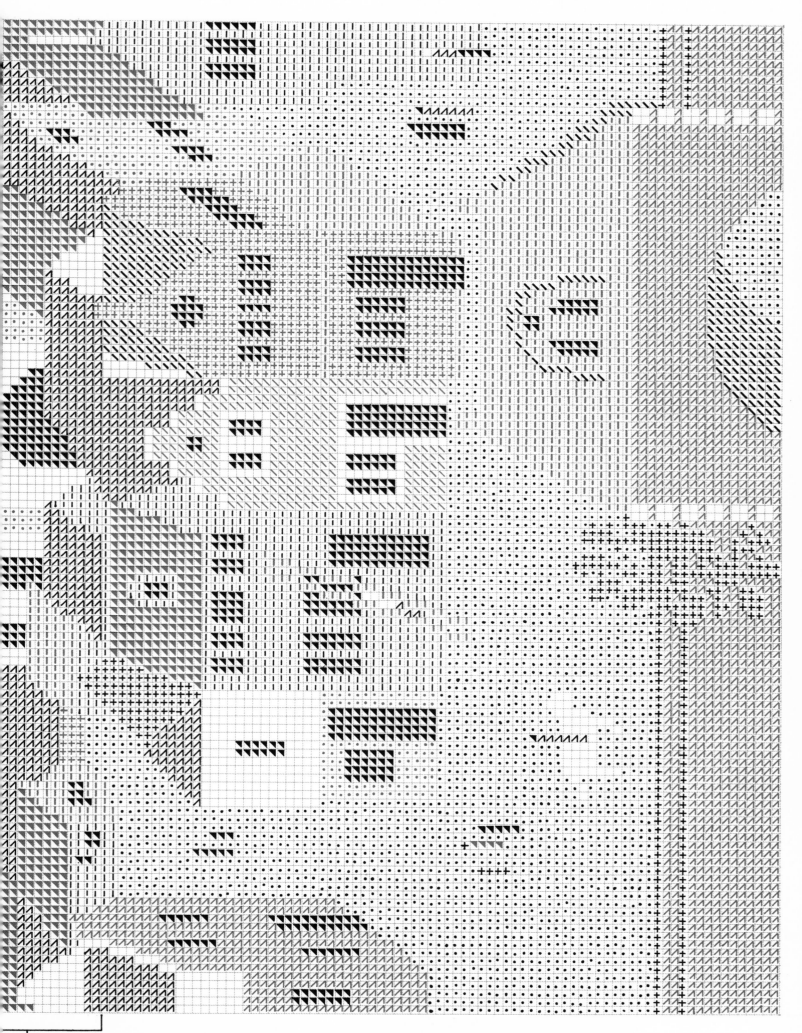

THIS PORTION OF THE GRAPH IS REPEATED.

THE UNICORN was believed to be a small, startlingly swift animal about the size of a young goat, with a sharp horn rising from his forehead. Supposedly immune from capture by hunters, he could be tricked into captivity, it was said, merely by placing a virgin nearby him. Upon noting her presence, the unicorn would promptly rush to her, climb delicately onto her lap and, for reasons that remain elusive, fall asleep. The Unicorn Tapestries, a series of seven woven hangings in The Cloisters, in New York, depict episodes in the hunt and capture of that elegant mythical beast. Probably woven in Brussels, a center for such work around 1500, the tapestries are filled with figures of hunters, noblemen, and their ladies, peasants, animals and over a hundred varieties of plants and trees.

Almost all of the flora have been depicted at the height of their beauty—the trees weighted with fruit, the flowers in full bloom— with no regard to the time of year in which each would normally blossom. A background so crammed with plants is referred to as *millefleurs* ("thousand flowers"), and each tapestry has a large section devoted to such *millefleurs* grounds.

The violets shown here are from the first tapestry, *The Start of the Hunt*. Though they are stylized and do not, perhaps, resemble precisely what we are used to seeing each April, they are immediately recognizable and charming in their simplicity. Violets, growing close to the earth, were a symbol of humility to medieval and Renaissance artists, and the Virgin was occasionally referred to as "the violet of humility."

ACTUAL SIZE 6" × 8½"

NAVY
LIGHT BLUE
MEDIUM BLUE
YELLOW
DARK GREEN
LIGHT GREEN
MEDIUM GREEN

149

□ ROSE
◣ BLACK
− YELLOW
✕ DARK GREEN
╱ LIGHT GREEN
• PALE YELLOW

THE LADY WITH THE UNICORN is a series of six tapestries from the Musée de Cluny in Paris executed toward the end of the fifteenth century. Like The Cloisters' Unicorn works, they depict human and animal figures against a *millefleurs* background. The predominant color in the Cluny hangings, unlike The Cloisters' dark blue ground, is a lovely, faded vermilion, similar to what is now called "rose madder." Indeed, the dyes that produced the soft, subtle hues of these tapestries came primarily from plants—madder for the reds, woad for the blues, and weld for yellow. Other shades were produced by mixing these dyes. The flower motif in this design is derived from the tapestry depicting Taste, one of the five senses illustrated in the series. In it, the Lady, with a parakeet on her gloved hand and the unicorn beside her, takes a sweetmeat from the dish held by her maid.

ACTUAL SIZE 7½" × 7⅜"

| RED
| BLACK
| WHITE
✕ GOLD
• BLACK
☐ WHITE

ANDREA DEL SARTO, the son of a Florentine tailor, painted the portrait of his wife, Lucrezia de Fede, from which this design was derived, early in the sixteenth century. A draped turban, striped like the pattern, is seen on her head.

The motif uses both tent and horizontal bargello stitches; woolen yarn may be substituted for the metallic yarn used here.

ACTUAL SIZE 7¼" × 5⅞"

THE UNICORN in this design is derived from a lace pattern, one of a collection published in 1587 as a book containing patterns for fancy stitchery (reprinted as *Renaissance Patterns for Lace and Embroidery*; New York: Dover Publications, 1971). The unicorn's horn, believed to possess powers of purification, particularly against arsenic, thus rendered nontoxic the water into which it was dipped.

In its religious context, the unicorn myth was interpreted as an allegory of the Annunciation and of the Incarnation of Christ, born of the Virgin Mary.

The design is copied almost exactly from the 1587 pattern, which looks remarkably like a needlepoint chart on graph paper. The particular kind of lace referred to was made on a backing of square netting and the squares were either left open or filled in with a darning stitch, a technique called *guipre d'art* or *opus filatorium*. Because the design was small, 10-mesh-to-the-inch canvas was used here.

ACTUAL SIZE 7¾" × 6⅞"

A LUXURIOUS DRESS FABRIC depicted by Agnolo Bronzino in his portrait *Eleonora of Toledo with her Son, Don Giovanni* (ca. 1545) is the basis of this design. The fabric appears to be a motif of orange and black velvet against a ground of white satin, the plush of the velvet deep enough to cast a shadow behind it. The dress was apparently prized by Eleonora, for not only did she sit for her portrait while wearing it, but it is also thought to have been her wedding dress. When her tomb was opened in 1857, it was found that she had chosen to be buried in it.

ACTUAL SIZE 9¼" × 10½"

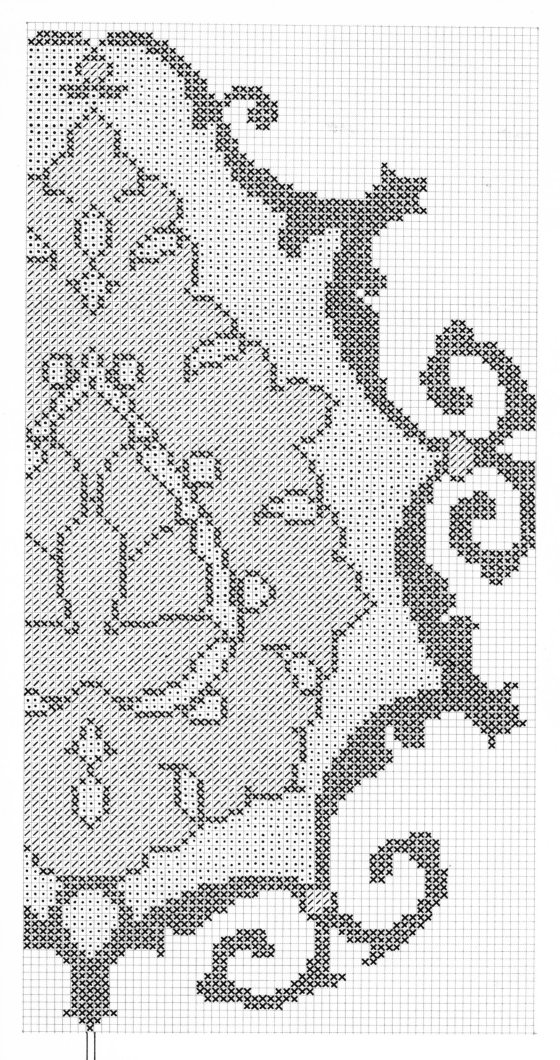

/ ORANGE

✕ BLACK

• WHITE

☐ PEACH

CENTER STITCH

IX DESIGNS FROM THE ART OF 17th–19th CENTURY EUROPE

THE COUNCIL OF TRENT, discharged in 1563, and the Counter Reformation it signaled helped to create a new religious iconography for the seventeenth century. Residence in Rome became the aspiration of young artists throughout Europe, lured by the large number of papal commissions. New scenes in the life of Christ—from his childhood, for example—and from the life of the Virgin were added to the artist's repertory. Nature was painted in an idealized fashion, with no stumps, dead branches, or any other imperfection.

Baroque artists, like those of the Renaissance, were enthralled by the possibilities of light, but their interpretations differed considerably from those of their predecessors. Natural light was no longer imitated on the painted surface, but rather imbued with added meaning in order to impart a mystical quality to the subject. Darkness became as important to the images as light itself in conveying and intensifying the symbolic nature of the subjects.

Painters who were granted large-scale commissions had to follow rigorous rules that dictated just how architecture, natural landscape elements, light-suffused atmosphere, and perspective were to be treated. Inspired by classical art, artists attempted to provide their patrons with pleasing variations of a prescribed visual environment. Also in vogue were scenes of everyday life—a sharp change from the mythological heroes or sacred figures that had provided the artistic fare for centuries. Whether farmers or gamblers, old men or infants, the new subjects were recognizable human beings engaged in activities that, as often as not, brought them joy. With their new independence, growing wealth, and the optimism they engendered, the Dutch began to collect these paintings, usually small-scale renderings, and thus encouraged the artists who sought to celebrate daily life. It must be remembered that the Dutch were Protestants, and partly as a reaction to the large-scale murals favored by the Catholic Churches, they turned to small intimate paintings which were suitable for contemplation in

the home. These works were bought at auction or from dealers, precursing the twentieth-century art marketplace.

In France, following the decision to centralize court life late in the seventeenth century, a former hunting lodge in Versailles, close to the capital, was expanded in order to house in suitable fashion the glittering nobility who clustered around the Sun King, Louis XIV. The focus of the palace was the garden, a space designed for contemplation from afar, not to be touched but to be looked at—a place where nature was as rigidly controlled in reality as it appeared to be in the court-commissioned paintings that decorated the palace's interiors. Versailles, with its splendid acres of marble and glass, was re-created spiritually in the rococo painting that followed the baroque era. The classical and ponderous baroque style gave way to a private, more frivolous kind of painting. The subjects were smaller, *intime*, and quiet. Love in its many manifestations was a frequent theme. This porcelained art, with its pretty details and smoky atmosphere, eventually descended to mere decoration. Artists soon began to look for larger, more inspiring themes, in keeping with the revolutionary spirit that had overturned a monarchy.

The artistic solution was found in a return to heroic painting in the classical style. The historical subjects had a contemporary political allusion that was widely understood by the cognoscenti. For example, in the *Death of Socrates* (1787) by Jacques-Louis David, the philosopher—a prefiguration and a personification of the Age of Reason—is seen as a Christ-like figure surrounded by twelve students as he accepts the cup of hemlock. To create superhuman effects, forms were delineated as if chiseled out of rock, with hard, smooth, polished surfaces; color was incidental, sometimes submerged wholly in graying tones with brushstrokes invisible on the painted surface. To the neoclassicists, drawing was the only meaningful element in a painting; color was just frosting on the cake.

Those less inclined to seize on contemporary history to make an artistic statement turned instead to nature. Powerful animals replaced men in exotic landscapes. The archaeological ruin, a memento mori and a symbol of man's creative aspirations, was a favorite subject of the romantic painters. The extraordinary moment in nature—a violent storm or a fight between animals—expressed the immanence of the supernatural.

The year 1860 was a watershed in the history of Western art. Artists began to turn away from politically earth-shaking events and the highly charged supernatural world to become intense observers of ordinary people enjoying an informal Sunday afternoon respite at water's edge. This relatively sedate group of Impressionists, as they came to be known, painted gay, lyrical scenes from unspectacular middle-class life. Fascinated by the sensation of luminosity, they went outdoors armed with small portable canvases to capture and convey the quality of light as reflected off the surface of water and the objects close by. Light was not manipulated in order to achieve an effect—they wanted only to record its reflections with fidelity at a particular time and place. Impressionist canvases are suffused with color and the energy conveyed by the artists' "handwriting"—the flickering effects of the brush as it applied the paint to the canvas.

The Impressionist movement, with its ephemeral, buoyant quality, was spurned by its artistic successors. No longer interested in observing and reproducing scenes from the life they saw around them, the newer artists attempted to project onto their canvases forms derived from their own psyches. Art became for them a means of delving into themselves, a way of searching for answers to the enigmas of life. Canvases became intensely emotional battlegrounds for the display of personal symbolism. Viewpoints changed radically, space became ambiguous, pigment was smeared on the canvas in an avalanche of anxiety.

In the last decade of the nineteenth century, a group of artists and writers attempted to create a synthesis of all the arts. The suggestive quality implicit in French Symbolist poetry and the influence of the flat asymmetry of Japanese wood-block prints were combined and translated by artist and artisan into the undulating lines possessed by plants and sea creatures. Known as Art Nouveau in England, where the style may have originated, the movement quickly spread throughout Europe and affected much of the painting produced during the period. Paul Gauguin, Henri de Toulouse-Lautrec, and Edvard Munch all manifested the effect of Art Nouveau on their work.

Little in the decorative arts remained untouched by it. From clothing to wallpaper, glassware, and architecture, the serpentine style reached out until it could be seen even on the labels of the foods one bought. By 1902 the effect had been diluted and cheapened so badly that it was dropped completely by its originators. The emergence, triumph, and sudden demise of the style had, however, laid the groundwork for the amazingly diverse, often startlingly transient artistic movements of the twentieth century.

PAINTER, SCULPTOR, AND ARCHITECT, Gianlorenzo Bernini frequently combined all of his gifts in the creation of works such as the Tomb of Alexander VII in St. Peter's in Rome. The dome of his Santa Maria dell' Assunzione, a church in Ariccia, executed between 1662 and 1664, with its hexagonal coffers, was the inspiration for this design. The coloring is invented, for the original coffers contain bronze rosettes and a bronze decorative edging that is represented here by a single silvery line.

ACTUAL SIZE 6" × 6"

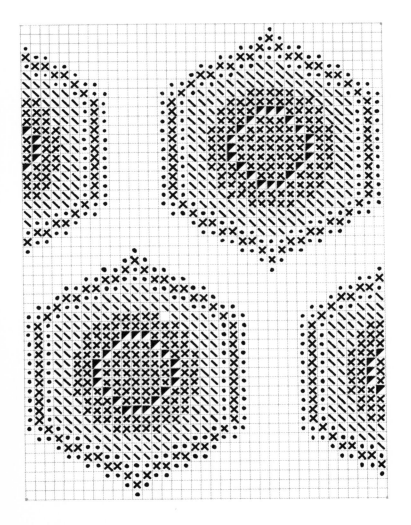

＼	LIGHT BLUE
✘	SILVER
◥	GRAY
☐	MEDIUM BLUE
•	WHITE

PETER PAUL RUBENS was an enormously successful Flemish artist as well as a sophisticated, well-traveled diplomat. At about the time of his marriage in 1609 to Isabella Brant, Rubens painted a portrait of himself and his bride. With clasped hands, they look confidently out at the viewer, rosy cheeked, well fed, and well dressed in their satin garments and lace collars.

The design shown here is an adaptation of a detail of the artist's jacket. The pale brown satin jacket was ornamented with black braid or embroidery in a kind of interlace evocative of wrought-iron grillwork. Though the pattern is cut off from the viewer by what appears to be the artist's cloak, it seems clear that the lines continued down to the waistline, and that is how they have been reproduced here.

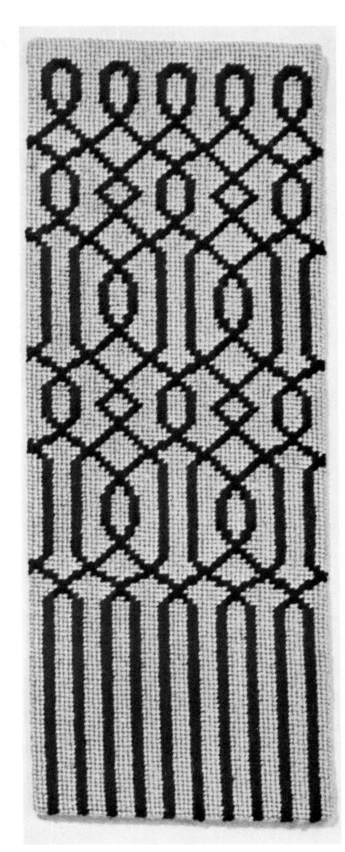

ACTUAL SIZE 4⅝″ × 12¾″

THE DOME was a frequent architectural element in seventeenth-century Italy. This design is a geometricized and simplified version of Guarino Guarini's dome of San Lorenzo in Turin, built between 1668 and 1687. Through Guarini's ingenious use of windows in the dome and its supporting members, the whole interior is suffused with light. The interplay of light and shadow inside the dome suggested this tonal color scheme.

ACTUAL SIZE 9" DIAMETER

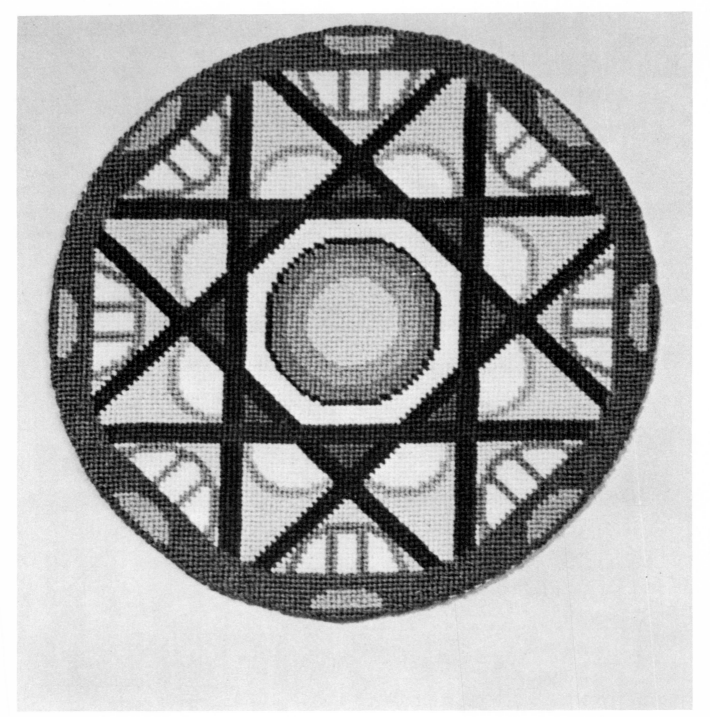

□ WHITE
• CREAM
— BEIGE
/ TAUPE
✕ BROWN
✛ GRAY

163

THE SALON DE VENUS at Versailles was decorated for Louis XIV by Charles Lebrun, court painter, founder of the Royal Academy of Arts and Sciences, and director of the Gobelins tapestry factory. The salon was one of six great rooms, each named for a planet that formed the *Grand appartement du reception du Roi*. The king's throne was placed in the room dedicated to the sun god, Apollo. The ceiling painting in the Salon de Venus is supposed to suggest the power of love on kings. The small design shown here is derived from the inlaid marble on the walls of the salon.

ACTUAL SIZE 2⅛″ × 14¾″

▲ RED

✕ GRAY

☐ WHITE

ACTUAL SIZE 10½" × 3¾"

THE INLAID MARBLE BASE of the sculpture complex known as the *Transparente*, completed in 1732 by Narciso Tomé, was the basis for this design. Located in the Cathedral in Toledo, Spain, the sculptural work contains many figures of Christ, the saints, and the prophets.

The design has been stitched in shades close to the originals and may be repeated in either length—in a belt, for example—or width (used three or four times for a pillow or a chair seat). The design is edged in a border of brick stitch for textural variety.

□ LIGHT GRAY
✗ DARK GRAY
• YELLOW
╱ RED
│ DARK GRAY

CENTER STITCH

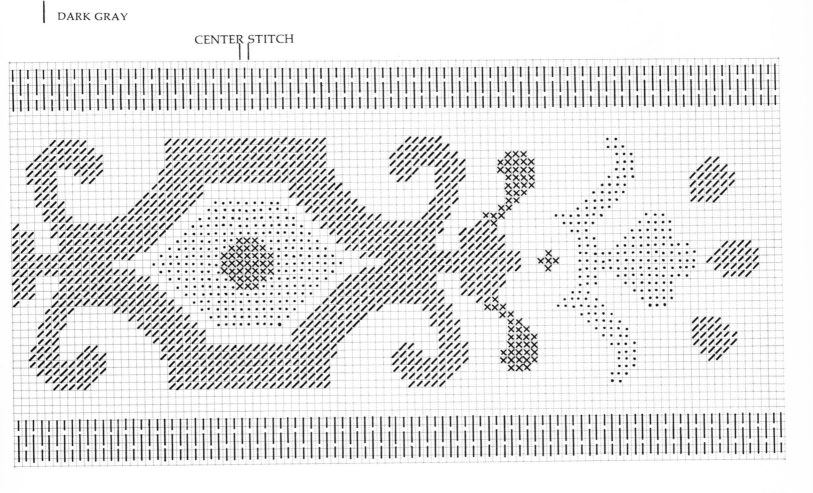

CENTER
STITCH

ACTUAL SIZE 8⅝" × 9½"

A MAZARINE was a pierced dish, a kind of strainer that fitted into a larger dish below it and was used to serve foods such as boiled fish. The design shown here is derived from such a fancifully pierced silver dish made in London in 1742 by John Le Sage.

THIS DELICATE FLORAL MOTIF is an adaptation from a glass paperweight made in France in the late 1840's. The producer of the paperweight was the Cristallerie de St. Louis, founded in 1767 and patronized by French royalty. Because the design is a tiny one, it was stitched on 10-mesh-to-the-inch canvas for greater visibility.

- • LIGHT GREEN
- ◤ NAVY
- ■ BLACK
- ✕ DARK GREEN
- + DARK RED
- ＼ DARK PINK
- — ORANGE
- ☐ TAUPE
- • WHITE
- ◤ BLUE
- ✕ MEDIUM GREEN
- + RED
- ＼ PINK
- — YELLOW

ACTUAL SIZE 7½″ × 8⅛″

167

IN 1896 the English architect Charles Annesley Voysey designed this wallpaper that he called the "Tulip and Bird." Although this paper and other wallpapers and fabrics by Voysey were inspired by the Art Nouveau style, their popularity continued until long after the period had ended early in the twentieth century.

In order to execute this pattern, outline the first tulip in the exact center of the canvas and proceed upward and downward from there. Because the pattern is symmetrical, it is a good deal easier to render than it may at first appear, since each element of the design is always the same number of threads away from the central tulip as its corresponding element on the other side. Check at frequent intervals when you outline (with a ruler, if necessary) to make sure that each side of the pattern balances the other.

Yellow has replaced the original background of pale blue-green in order to add a strong contrast and help set the pattern in greater relief.

ACTUAL SIZE 9¾" × 12¾"

CENTER
STITCH

□ YELLOW

• LIGHT GREEN

▼ BLUE-GRAY

✕ VIOLET

+ TURQUOISE

\ LIGHT BLUE

THE CREATORS of this motif, taken from a porcelain jug made in England about 1860, turned to the past for inspiration—a pattern based on ornamentation typical of the Renaissance. The metallic glint of the original gilding was replaced in this needlepoint adaptation with a woolen dark-gold yarn.

On the jug, the circular, leafy pattern was placed between two bands of light red and green, although there is only one here. If desired, the original pattern can be duplicated by executing the design as charted here, by placing the white and gold band in the center of the canvas, stitching the red and green one immediately below it (as indicated in the chart), and then turning the canvas around and repeating the red and green band on the other side of the white and gold one.

ACTUAL SIZE 6¼" × 6"

| GREEN
• GOLD
□ WHITE
✕ RED
╲ GREEN

THE ART NOUVEAU movement in Germany was known as Jugendstil, after the Munich weekly magazine *Die Jugend*. Among the artists whose work appeared in *Die Jugend* was Otto Eckmann, a landscape painter turned designer. Though known for his depictions of floral forms, Eckmann also designed furniture and metal work and made contributions to graphic art. He designed an alphabet that became the most popular of all of the Art Nouveau typefaces, and for the Rudhard Type Foundry he created around 1900 the decorative border shown here.

The original colors for the motif would, of course, be black and white. The orange and purple used here were inspired by an advertising poster of the period.

ACTUAL SIZE 7¼" × 2¾"

X DESIGNS INSPIRED BY AMERICAN FOLK ART

MOST OF the early settlers on the new continent of America had been unable to bring many of life's necessities with them across the ocean. The habit of making do with one's own household goods, particularly where neighbors were few and distant, was thus instilled almost immediately. Imported merchandise was too costly for most Americans, moreover, and before an object was brought into the small, crowded homes of the pioneers, its utility generally had to be apparent. There was scant opportunity for frivolity; demands on time were unending, the seasons were inexorable, and leisure was a precious commodity in a frontier land. American art and craft were slow, then, to come to life.

As the colonies spread, towns multiplied, and farming improved, carpenters, smiths, and other artisans, freed from the necessity of growing food, were able to devote themselves to their vocations. Often unschooled, these craftsmen had learned their trades from their elders, who taught them decorative traditions along with the mechanical operations. As commerce and manufactures grew, households became more secure and the need for strict utility in every purchased item was diminished. The first luxury goods began to come to market.

The simple furniture in most early American homes was often embellished at least modestly, perhaps carved or painted, and to enliven the plain plaster walls, the art of stenciling was revived in New England. A stencil is a sheet of parchment, paper, or tin with a design cut out of it so that when a pigment or dye is rubbed over the opening, the design is reproduced on the surface below—a time-saving technique used for centuries in Europe and the Orient. Wallpaper, made in France or England, was too expensive for most homes, and stencils were a less costly substitute. Then, too, walls did not need the extensive preparation for stenciling that they did for wallpapers, nor did patterns have to be matched.

Most of the stencil designs that have been saved and recorded date from the first quarter of the nine-teenth century and were rendered in New England, although some of the work has been found as far away as Ohio. Many of the early stencilers were itinerant artists, working in homes as they traveled and employing a stock of designs that was occasionally augmented by borrowing from others. Design sources varied, but favorites were plant and geometrical motifs, hearts, stars, eagles, fans, and drapery. Though stenciling was occasionally done in a single shade, as many as four colors might be used in any one design, with a different stencil for each color. Black, green, yellow, and shades of red were most common, placed on grounds of yellow and red ochers, blue, and rose —cheerful additions to the unadorned rooms in small farmhouses.

Nearly from the first, almost every home contained a loom for weaving much of the cloth worn by early Americans. Coverlets, too, often made of linen and wool, were woven on simple, four-harness looms, since flax and wool were staple farm products in the colonies. A loom attachment invented by Joseph Jacquard, a Frenchman, mechanized the weaving process and permitted a variety of patterns to be woven into a single piece of goods. Imported to the United States in 1820, the attachment employed a series of punched cards, not unlike those used in modern computers, to raise and lower the harnesses, which by then numbered as many as forty. Weavers were able to design large coverlets individually, often incorporating names, dates, and places in the borders of the designs, while the centers contained repetitions of geometricized flower-like forms. Commemorative coverlets were executed to celebrate events as diverse as the opening of a railroad or the nation's centennial.

While there was little need in modest American homes for ornamental sculpture, the woodcarver was able to find a functional outlet in the creation of weathervanes, a necessity for every farmer's barn. Placed at the peak of the roof and silhouetted against the sky, the weathervane served as a forecaster as it shifted slowly with the prevailing wind, portending changes in the weather. Other uses for the wood-carver's skill during the nineteenth century were in the creation of ships' figureheads and sternboards, cigar-store figures, and, most endearing of all, children's toys.

Long before the British conceived of colonizing the New World, they had become expert needleworkers. Manor-house interiors were damp, drafty places, and for all but the very few at the top of the economic ladder, it was financially impossible to purchase the splendid tapestries, draperies, and oriental carpets that might provide insulation against the chill. Since most of these homes and their domains were forced to be economically self-sustaining, the job of manufacturing suitable embroidered goods fell to the women of each household. Trained in the needle arts since childhood, Englishwomen of the sixteenth and seventeenth centuries executed exquisite embroideries, some of which still survive. The granddaughters of those women migrated to the colonies and used the skills learned in their youth for the decorative embellishment of their American homes. Many of the needlework patterns used to upholster early American furniture are derived from English prototypes.

In few eighteenth- and nineteenth-century homes, though, did women have the time to fashion upholstery fabric for a single chair. Other chores and needs were far more pressing. But at the end of the day, when the light had faded and other work had been put aside, women were fond of sitting by the fireside and turning their skill at stitchery to the piecing of always needed quilts. Fabric, especially early in the nineteenth century, was expensive, and outworn garments were cut apart for the salvageable bits and pieces. When enough pieces were saved, women planned out their quilts, calculating sizes and shades of available materials. Then, with the use of templates, or patterns made of tin, or perhaps heavy paper, the pieces of the quilt were cut and assembled, and the long process of stitching was begun.

Patchwork quilts were made in either of two techniques—appliqué, in which pieces of fabric were cut out and sewn onto another piece used as a backing, and piecework, in which sections of fabric were sewn together to make the square or rectangular blocks that were joined to create the quilt tops. The appliqué quilt, which needed new fabric for its backing, tended to be used for "show." The pieced quilt was the more economical, since no new fabric had to be used in its construction, and had the added advantage of being "lapwork"; it was easier to put together than the bulky yardage of the appliquéd type because the small pieces could be joined until a block or square of the desired size was completed. Most of these quilts were functional furnishings meant to withstand hard use; those that have survived were generally put away for posterity.

As the country expanded westward, quilts were taken along in the wagons, and patterns moved across the country, too. At fairs, quilts were exhibited and exchanged, and women were able to find new patterns to increase their collections. Though many quilt patterns resemble the tile arrangements of Roman and Byzantine floors, it is thought that these geometric designs were not copied, but were re-invented in America. The quilting bee, where quilt tops, batting, and lining were sewn together by a group, was a social institution that permitted isolated women to share their work and a bit of gossip in the process. Beauty and history were stitched into many a quilt, along with the unspoken narrative of family failures and dreams.

A NOT UNCOMMON FEATURE of household decoration in the eighteenth and early nineteenth centuries was stenciling on walls and furniture. This design, dated around 1824, is derived from a stencil pattern found in the home of Josiah Sage in South Sandisfield, Massachusetts. It has been reproduced on 10-mesh-to-the-inch canvas in colors close to, but undoubtedly brighter than, the originals.

ACTUAL SIZE 6¾" × 6¾"

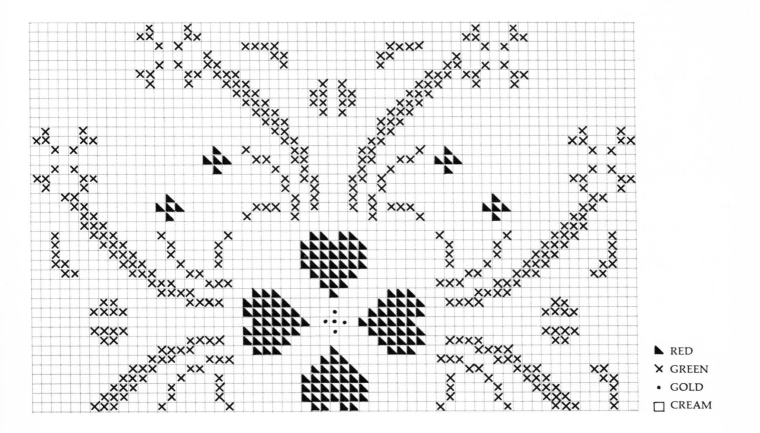

▲ RED
✕ GREEN
• GOLD
☐ CREAM

175

	PALE YELLOW		CHARCOAL GRAY		LIGHT RED
	DARK YELLOW		LIGHT GREEN		MEDIUM RED
	MEDIUM YELLOW		MEDIUM GREEN		DARK RED
			DARK GREEN		

A LARGE WING CHAIR, probably dating from the first half of the eighteenth century, served as the source for this bargello-work design, which recalls a seventeenth-century English carnation pattern. The chair, now in the Metropolitan Museum of Art in New York, is embroidered in the back in a completely different pattern, a landscape composition including flowers, trees, and animals.

The red and yellow, which appear to have been randomly placed in the original, have been regularized in this adaptation. The use of a single color in combination with the greens would produce an equally appealing effect.

The easiest way to execute this pattern is to work the dark gray lines of stitches first and then proceed with the flower forms, starting with the dark green at the base of the calyx and working upward. The green lines at the tops of the flowers can be done last.

ACTUAL SIZE 13⅝" × 11½"

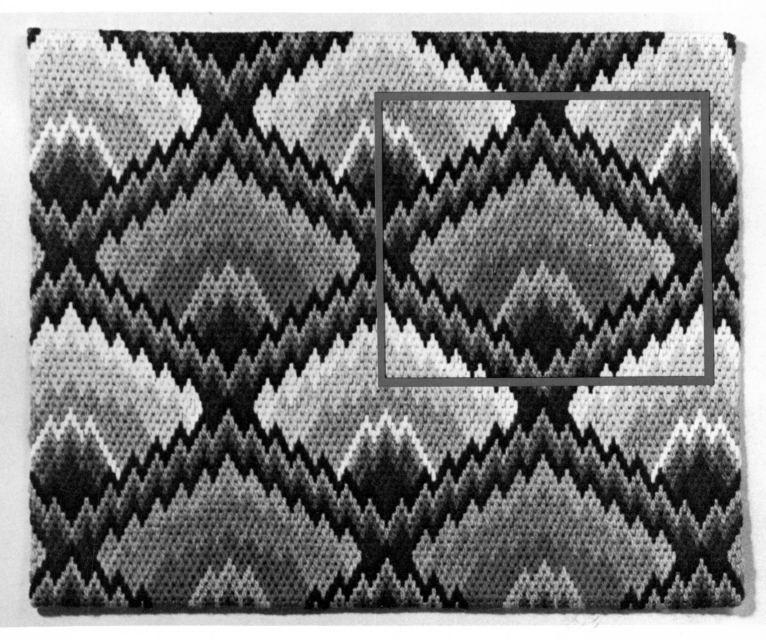

TOP

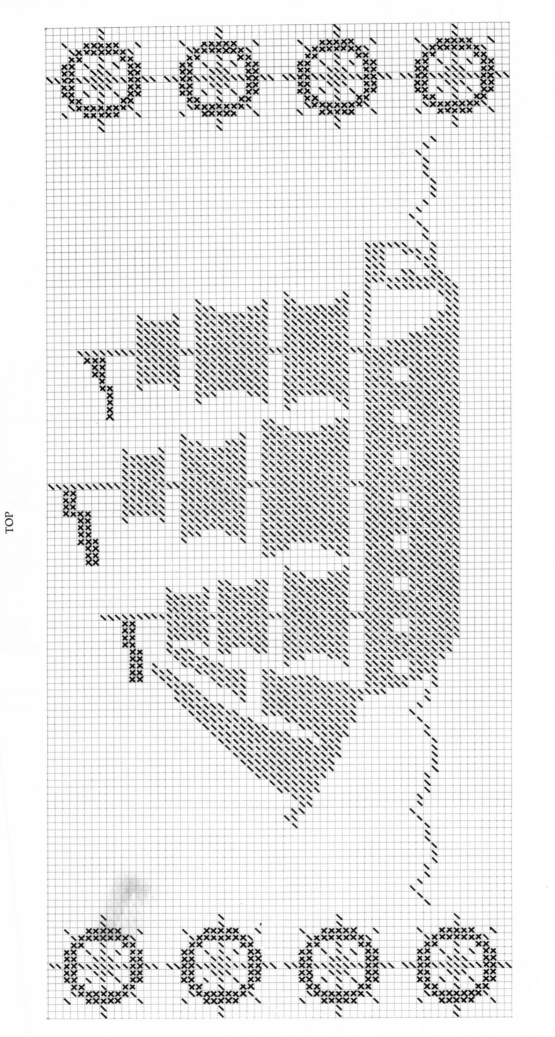

BLUE
RED
WHITE

THE COVERLET WEAVER frequently celebrated the events of his time by memorializing them in his work. This clipper ship was a small monument to the men who sailed the oceans pursuing the "China trade," for it is included in a scene depicting both Boston harbor and the ship's eventual destination—a Chinese town with pagodas and palm trees. Made about 1840, and now in the Henry Ford Museum, Dearborn, Michigan, the coverlet is actually just blue and white; the red is an invention, as are the wheels that serve to border the ship. The design was executed on 10-mesh-to-the-inch canvas.

ACTUAL SIZE 14⅛" × 6¼"

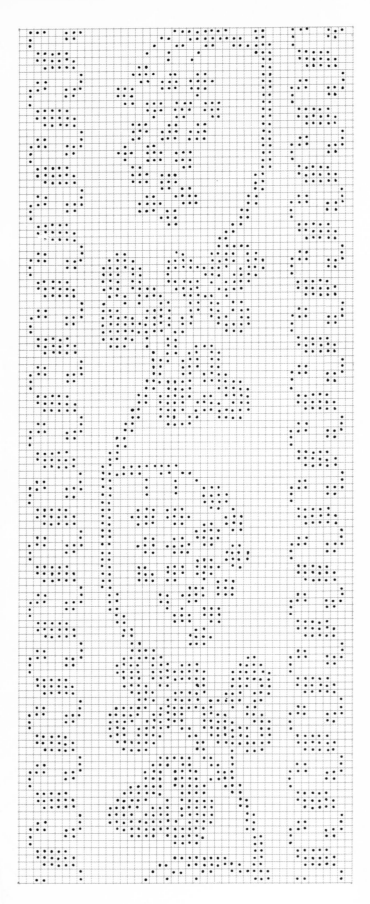

BOTH BEAUTIFUL and productive, the grapevine has been a favorite motif for centuries. The version shown here was used by a coverlet maker in about 1840 to border his work. The central panel contained depictions of pagodas and palm trees, churches and farmhouses, that came to be known as the "Christian and Heathen" motif and was included as a border on some later coverlets. The original colors were blue and white.

ACTUAL SIZE 3½" × 11"

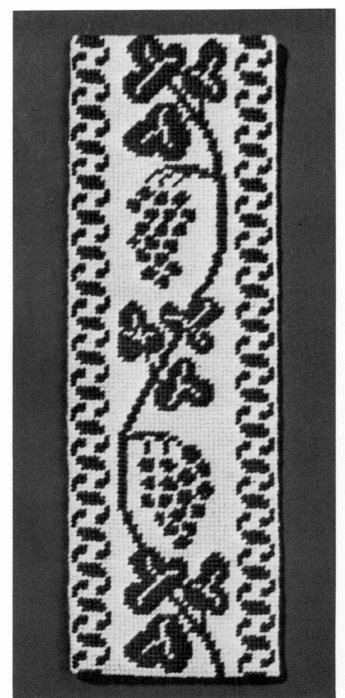

TO EARLY AMERICANS, the pineapple was a symbol of hospitality that frequently ornamented furniture. The fruit, with its spiny, overlapping leaves, inspired a pieced-quilt pattern that became the basis for this bargello design. Now in the Metropolitan Museum of Art, the quilt dates from the last quarter of the nineteenth century and is believed to have been made in Pennsylvania by the Amish or Mennonites. The shades used here are close to the original.

The bargello stitches that form the sides of the motif are not difficult to work, but it is necessary to be careful when counting them. The motif in the center of the square is based on a variation of the scotch stitch. The enlargement of the motif on the chart indicates just how the stitches are to be executed. It is basically a diagonal arrangement of bargello stitches that form a sort of diamond pattern. Again, care should be taken in counting the number of canvas threads that are covered in each stitch, but once the motif has been done, repetitions become increasingly easier.

ACTUAL SIZE 7⅛" × 7⅛"

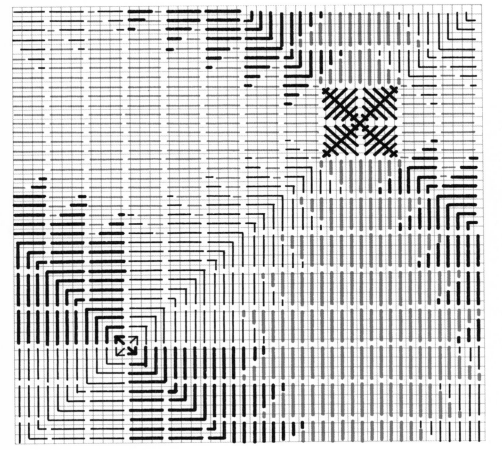

	BROWN
	GREEN
	RED
	YELLOW

DETAIL

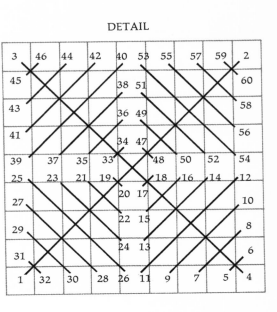

Needle out of canvas at odd numbers, needle into canvas at even numbers.

181

MOST CITY SCENES portrayed on coverlets were referred to as "True Boston Town" patterns, probably because the first such pattern was an attempt to depict that city. In any case, this townscape of 1848, originally woven in blue and white, is a charming example of an idealized skyline.

The pattern consists of five building elements that are reversed and can be repeated indefinitely. The chart shows only these elements, but a comparison of sample and chart will reveal that, reading from right to left, the second group of buildings is just a mirror image of the first four.

ACTUAL SIZE 16⅝" × 6¾"

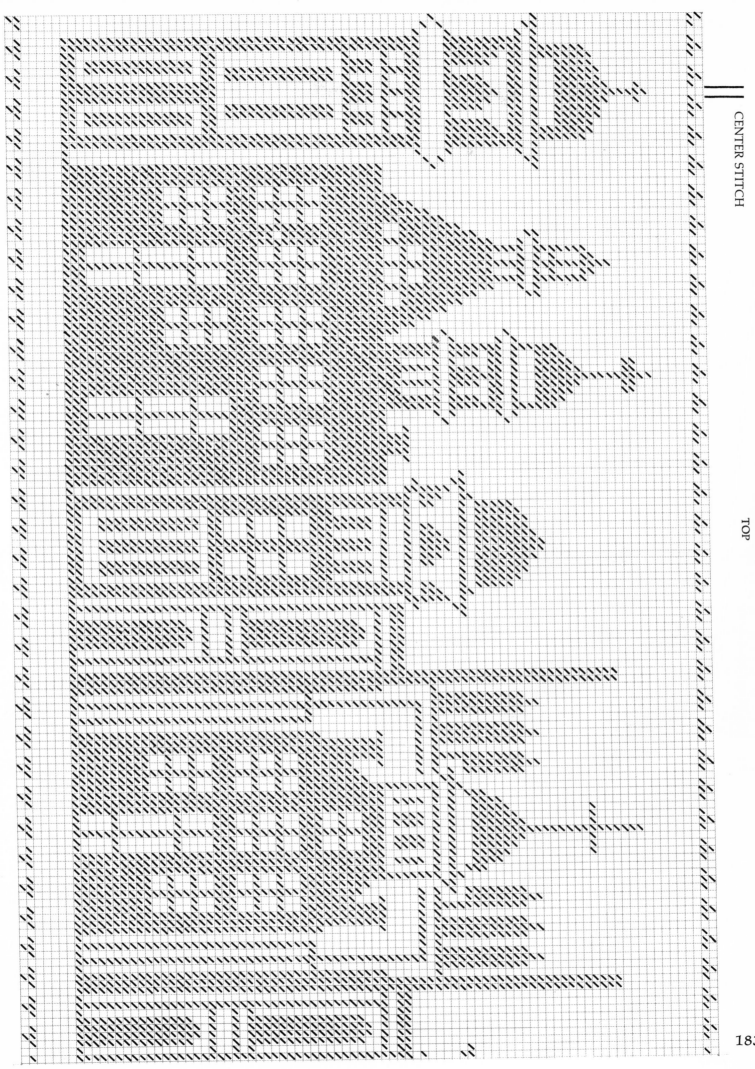

TOP

THE ADVENT OF THE RAILROAD provided coverlet weavers with a popular new subject. This engine
and wood-car, including its number, were used as a
border motif in a coverlet of 1850 to commemorate
the Hemfield Railroad. Just where the railroad ran,
unfortunately, is not known—but not very far and
not very fast, from the looks of it.

The weaver, probably possessed of a mechanical
bent, incorporated the spool-shaped piston and rod
that drove the rear wheel, normally an interior mech-
anism, into his drawing of the locomotive's exterior,
perhaps to indicate just what was going on inside.
The coverlet was woven in red, navy, and white and
is in a private collection.

ACTUAL SIZE 11⅜″ × 5¼″

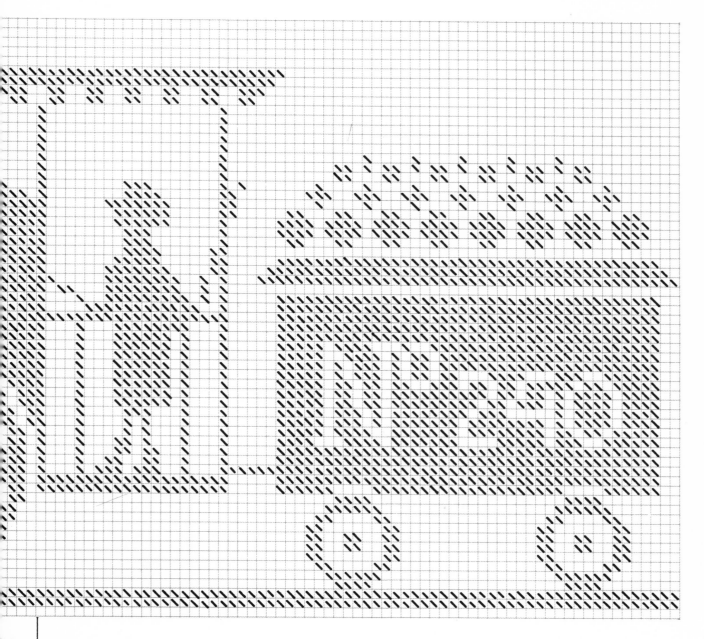

PORTION OF THE GRAPH IS REPEATED.

185

TOP

THE WEATHERVANE was of importance to all who made their living off the land or sea, since a shift in the wind might portend a change in the weather. The anonymous wood carver who around 1875 executed the weathervane upon which this design is based seems to have paid scant attention to the proportions of the Indian; however, the horse was beautifully observed and its thrust strongly rendered. The carver's sure eye for detail is seen in the way the feathers in the Indian's headband are echoed in the points of the horse's mane and tail.

This weathervane design is executed in shades that may have been seen when the object was silhouetted against the sky. It is from the collection of American folk-art scholars Howard and Jean Lipman, and was included in the exhibition "The Flowering of American Folk Art, 1776–1876" at the Whitney Museum of American Art in 1974.

ACTUAL SIZE 11" × 9⅜"

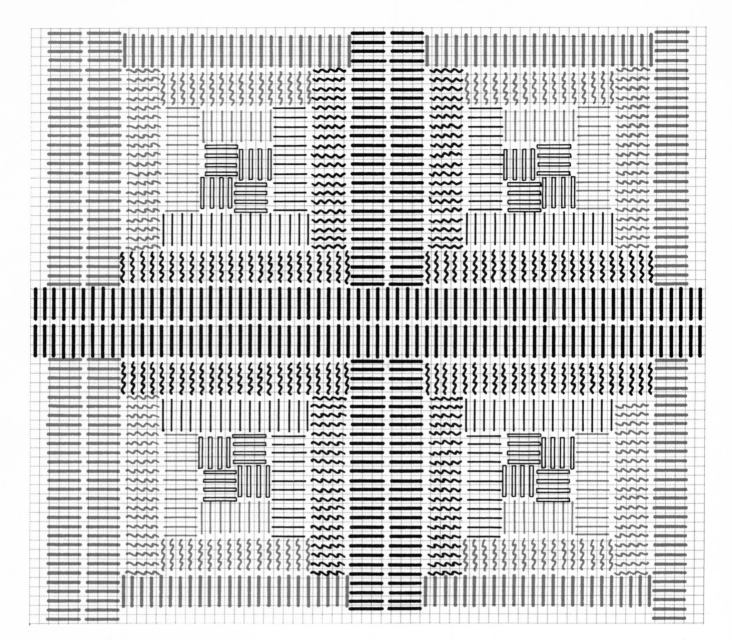

DARK BLUE

MEDIUM BLUE

LIGHT BLUE

RED

PALE YELLOW

MEDIUM YELLOW

DARK YELLOW

COVERLETS based on the principle of strips of fabric sewn parallel to the sides of a central square to form small blocks are called Log Cabin quilts. The central square was often red or yellow, and light and dark fabric strips were often arranged around the center in varying ways so that, when completed, the quilt might present one of a number of favored *trompe l'oeil* designs.

In this bargello design, based on such Log Cabin quilts, the dark and light fabric strips are here represented by blue and yellow tones around the red square. When completed, this particular pattern forms a series of light and dark lozenges.

As with other bargello designs in this collection, two stitches will often enter the same opening so that the canvas is completely covered, as can be seen on the chart. Care must also be taken to count stitches correctly or the pattern will be thrown off, for there are instances in which two blocks share the same stitch between them. Fortunately, once one whole block is completed, additional ones are considerably easier. It is probably more convenient to begin working at one corner of the canvas and add blocks of design next to the first one, and then below or above the first, working the blocks from the exterior toward the center and completing one shade at a time.

ACTUAL SIZE 9¼" × 9⅛"

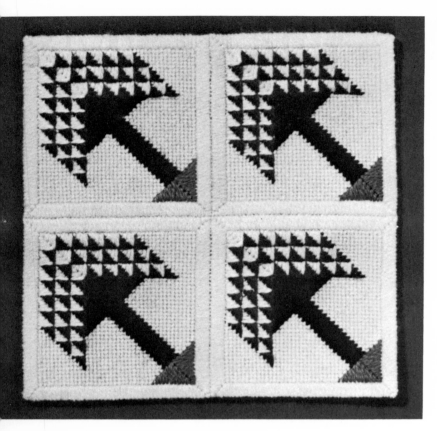

THE TREE OF LIFE, or sacred tree, has an artistic lifespan of thousands of years. From the residents of ancient Mesopotamia, to Persian craftsmen, to the chintz makers of India who exported their goods to Western Europeans, the symbol persisted until it was adapted for the patchwork of the American quiltmaker, who connected it to the religious concept of eternal life. Widely used during the last half of the nineteenth century, this variety of quilt often combined both techniques—pieced work in the leaves and appliqué for the trunk and background. The colors of the sample are the ones often used in this quilt pattern.

As in many patterns where long bargello and short continental stitches are used, it is best to do the bargello first and gently lift the yarn so that the continental stitches can slide in beneath them.

ACTUAL SIZE 7⅛" × 7⅛"

	ROSE
	WHITE
	GREEN
	BROWN

190

Bibliographical Note

The short historical essays offered in this book to orient the reader are, of course, a product of many sources and many hours passed in the classroom, libraries, museums, and in personal observation. A list of works consulted, therefore, would be both extensive and pretentious. If the reader's interest in art history is quickened by the abbreviated sketches here and he or she wishes to delve more deeply into the matter, the most recent edition of H. W. Janson's *History of Art* (New York, Abrams) and its bibliography are suggested as a starting place.

Among the many needlepoint primers in existence, those that the author has found helpful are:

Caulfield, Sophia A. F., and Saward, Blanche C. *The Dictionary of Needlework.* New York: Arno Press, 1972. (Facsimile of 1882 edition.)

Hanley, Hope. *Needlepoint.* New York: Scribner's, 1964.

Snook, Barbara. *Florentine Embroidery.* New York: Scribner's, 1967.

Williams, Elsa S. *Bargello, Florentine Canvas Work.* New York: Reinhold Publishing, 1967.

The following books are useful for learning about American folk art:

Holstein, Jonathan. *The Pieced Quilt: An American Design Tradition.* Greenwich, Conn.: New York Graphic Society, 1973.

Lipman, Jean. *American Folk Art in Wood, Metal and Stone.* New York: Dover Publications, 1972.

Lipman, Jean, and Winchester, Alice. *The Flowering of American Folk Art, 1776–1876.* New York: Viking, 1974.

Safford, Carleton L., and Bishop, Robert. *America's Quilts and Coverlets.* New York: Dutton, 1972.

Waring, Janet. *Early American Stencils on Walls and Furniture.* New York: Dover Publications, 1968.

A NOTE ABOUT THE TYPE

The text of this book was set in Palatino, a type face designed by the noted German typographer Hermann Zapf. Named after Giovanbattista Palatino, a writing master of Renaissance Italy, Palatino was the first of Zapf's type faces to be introduced to America. The first designs for the face were made in 1948, and the fonts for the complete face were issued between 1950 and 1952. Like all Zapf-designed type faces, Palatino is beautifully balanced and exceedingly readable.

The book was composed by Hallmark Press Inc., New York City; printed by Rae Publishing Company, Cedar Grove, New Jersey; bound by American Book-Stratford Press, Saddle Brook, New Jersey

All photographs, color and monochrome: Otto Maya
Graphs: Jill Weber
Text design and production supervision: Helen Barrow